KOREA LAW 101

BASIC AND PRACTICAL KNOWLEDGE FOR FOREIGN LAWYERS AND ENTREPRENEURS

JINNY SUH

ISBN: 979-8-311-44890-1

Printed in the United States of America

Disclaimer: This book is for informational purposes only and does not constitute legal advice. The views expressed are solely those of the author and do not represent the opinions, positions, or policies of any current or former employer. Readers should consult a qualified legal professional for specific legal matters.

OPENING

When I began my legal career in 2007, fresh out of law school, it became clear that academic theories barely prepared me for the realities of legal practice. Over the past 18 years, I've gained practical insights into the skills lawyers actually need to work in Korea—skills rarely addressed in textbooks.

I am licensed to practice in both Korea and the United States. My U.S. training and bar admission provided a strong academic foundation, but my practical experience there is limited to law school and the bar exam. In Korea, however, I built my career through hands-on work—advising clients at Kim & Chang, running my own legal practice, and handling corporate legal issues as in-house counsel at a global consulting firm. This dual perspective led me to ask: if I suddenly needed to practice in the U.S., where I have education but little practical experience, what kind of resource would I need? This book is the answer, written for foreign lawyers navigating Korean legal matters.

This is not an academic book. It avoids theoretical discussions and case analyses, focusing instead on practical guidance. It is written for professionals entering roles such as a foreign lawyer at a prominent Korean firm, an in-house attorney at a large Korean company, or a lawyer managing Korean clients at a multinational firm. For anyone in these situations, this book offers a clear entry point.

By the end of this book, readers will have a comprehensive overview of Korean law and its judicial and administrative systems. It provides guidance on finding key resources such as statutes, case precedents, corporate filings, and contract templates, as well as understanding the structure and process of investigations and litigation. The focus is on actionable insights, offering clarity and utility over abstract discussions.

For foreign lawyers working in Korea or advising Korean clients, this book serves as a toolkit. It is designed to save time, simplify the learning process, and support success in legal practice, whether drafting an NDA for a Korean subsidiary or advising on a cross-border transaction.

CONTENTS

CHAPTER 1.
THE FRAMEWORK AND STATUTES

SECTION 1. THE CIVIL LAW SYSTEM

LET'S GO BACK to law school. There are largely two types of legal system: the Civil Law system and the Common Law system. Just like switching from Google map to Naver map requires adapting to a new interface, understanding these legal systems is about learning how they each present information.

Korea operates under the **Civil Law system**, which differs fundamentally from the **Common Law system** of the U.S. Let's explore the essence of the Civil Law system that shapes Korea's legal framework and compare it with its Common Law counterpart.

CIVIL LAW VS. COMMON LAW: A BRIEF DISTINCTION

In the Civil Law system, legal decisions rely primarily on written codes and statutes. Think of it like following a map where every route and direction is carefully marked. Countries like Korea, Japan, and Germany rely on detailed, comprehensive legal codes to provide clear guidelines for governance and dispute resolution. By contrast, **Common Law systems**, as seen in the U.S. and the U.K., function like evolving maps. They change and grow with each judicial decision, as case laws derived from court rulings—creates new paths over time. A landmark case is like a traveler discovering a new route, redrawing the map to reflect the changing landscape.

In essence, the Civil Law system, which governs Korea, places statutes at the heart of every legal inquiry. Just as a map designed for New York won't help you navigate Seoul's alleys, legal strategies suited to a Common Law system might need to be adjusted for Korea's statute-driven legal framework.

CIVIL LAW VS. COMMON LAW: PRACTICAL REALITIES

Despite these differences, it's important to note that precedents in Korea, while not legally binding as in Common Law countries, still hold substantial practical significance. For instance, when a public official takes measures to enforce a statute, their official guide is the written law. Yet, in practice, they often look at how similar cases were previously managed, ensuring their decisions align with established practices. This method, somewhat akin to a traveler consulting both a detailed map and the experiences of those who have traveled the road before, ensures a consistent and practical application of the law.

Similarly, in Common Law countries like the U.S., statutes and regulations—such as the United States Code (USC) and Code of Federal Regulations (CFR)—are as important as case law. In practice, the Korean system, though rooted in statutes, achieves outcomes that often align with familiar legal approaches used in Common Law countries. Understanding this blend of written law and practical precedent makes the Korean legal system feel more accessible than it may first appear to lawyers trained in Common Law jurisdictions.

Bullet Point Summary

- **Korea's Legal Framework**: Korea follows the Civil Law system, relying on written statutes as the primary source of law, unlike Common Law systems that evolve through case law.
- **Practical Application**: Although precedents are not legally binding, they hold practical significance, helping officials and legal practitioners apply statutes consistently, often producing outcomes similar to those in Common Law jurisdictions.

SECTION 2. MAJOR WRITTEN STATUTES

THE EXPANSIVE REALM OF KOREAN STATUTES

HAVING EXPLORED THE distinction between the Civil Law and Common Law systems, we now shift focus to Korea's legal framework. As a Civil Law country, Korea's legal system is built on an extensive collection of written codes and statutes.

Korea's legal framework is remarkably vast, housing an impressive 1,825 laws according to the National Assembly Law Information as of January 29, 2024 (7,287 if considering the number of Enforcement Rule(시행령) and Enforcement Decree (시행규칙)). This number reflects the depth and detail of Korean law. To put it into perspective, there's even a law named "2023 Saemangeum World Scout Jamboree Support Special Act"(2023 새만금 세계스카우트 잼버리 지원 특별법), specifically enacted to facilitate the 25th World Scout Jamboree. This breadth demonstrates the granularity of Korea’s legal framework, making it challenging even for experienced lawyers to be familiar with every regulation.

NAVIGATING THE CORE STATUTES

The sheer number of laws in Korea, totaling 1,825 as noted by the National Assembly Law Information as of January 29, 2024, might initially seem daunting. However, like navigating a complex network of roads with the guidance of major highways, focusing on key legal codes can simplify this journey. One practical approach is to begin with the key legal codes tested on the Korean Bar Exam, including the Civil Act, the Criminal Act, and the Commercial Act. Much like medical or business school, where students are taught fundamental theories and principles that may not be directly applied in day-to-day practice but form the framework for understanding the field, these legal codes serve a similar purpose. They lay the groundwork for legal understanding, providing a base upon which practical legal advisory and practice are built, even if the day-to-day application diverges from these foundational studies.

▪ Civil Act(민법)

The Civil Act governs personal and property relationships between private parties. It covers a wide range of issues, including property ownership, contracts, torts, family law, and inheritances, similar to how the **Restatements of the Law** in the U.S. offer a comprehensive summary of common law principles in these areas. This Act lays the foundation for civil law in Korea, establishing the basic legal framework for private rights and duties.

▪ Commercial Act(상법)

The Commercial Act establishes the legal framework for business transactions and corporate entities. It addresses company formation, operation, and dissolution, similar to how the **Uniform Commercial Code (UCC)** functions in the U.S. Understanding this Act is essential for navigating Korea's business environment, as it governs both commercial activities and corporate governance.

▪ **Criminal Act (형법)**

The Criminal Act outlines the definitions of criminal offenses and penalties. It serves as the basis for enforcing public order and protecting citizens by defining criminal behavior and legal repercussions. This is similar to the **Model Penal Code (MPC)** in the U.S., which serves as a standardized, though not universally adopted, set of criminal law guidelines for states.

▪ **Constitution (헌법)**

The Constitution is the supreme law of Korea, outlining the structure of the government, the rights of citizens, and the fundamental principles of the state. It serves as the cornerstone of legal order and guarantees fundamental rights and freedoms.

▪ **Administrative Law (행정법)**

Administrative law governs the organization and operation of government agencies and their interactions with the public. Similar to the **Administrative Procedure Act (APA)** in the U.S., it provides a framework for transparent administrative actions and citizen protections. Unlike other Acts covered in this Section, there isn't a single statute titled 'Administrative Law'. Instead, it encompasses a collection of interrelated statutes, each fulfilling distinct roles within the administrative legal framework. These statutes include the **General Act on Public Administration (행정기본법)** and **Framework Act on Administrative Regulation (행정규제기본법)** prescribing the basic concepts and principles of administrative action and regulations. **Administrative Procedures Act (**행정절차법) delineates the procedural requirements for government agencies when making administrative decisions, while the **Administrative Litigation Act (행정소송법)** governs the procedures for resolving disputes arising from administrative decisions through litigation in administrative courts. Together, these statutes constitute the foundation of Administrative Law in Korea, ensuring procedural fairness, accountability, and the protection of citizens' rights in their interactions with government agencies.

▪ **Civil Procedure Act (민사소송법)**

The Civil Procedure Act outlines procedures for civil litigation, guiding the process from filing a lawsuit to enforcing judgments. It mirrors the U.S. Federal Rules of Civil Procedure, ensuring fair and efficient resolution of civil disputes.

▪ **Criminal Procedure Act (형사소송법)**

This Act governs criminal prosecutions, detailing procedures from investigation to trial and appeal. Similar to the **U.S. Federal Rules of Criminal Procedure**, it ensures that the rights of the accused are protected while maintaining public safety and justice.

It's worth noting that, once in practice, the focus shifts. In my experience as a transaction attorney and in-house counsel, I rarely needed to consult the Constitution, Administrative Law, or Criminal Procedure. Instead, the real focus in practice falls on specialized statutes not heavily emphasized in law school. These include the Monopoly Regulation and Fair Trade Act, Labor Standards Act, Personal Information Protection Act, Copyright Act, Unfair Competition Prevention and Trade Secret Protection Act, and Financial Investment Services and Capital Markets Act—all of which we will explore in the next section.

THE REAL CORE STATUTES

After completing law school and passing the bar exam, many quickly realize that much of what they studied has limited direct application in practice. The statutes that each legal counsel focuses on depend heavily on their industry, role, and specific legal domain. For instance, an in-house counsel at a pharmaceutical company will emphasize pharmaceutical regulations, while a privacy officer prioritizes data protection laws. Attorneys working in financial services are more likely to focus on capital markets and securities regulations. In practice, the "core statutes" you encounter are dictated by the specific demands of your work. This section draws on my experience to illustrate how practical legal work diverges from theoretical legal education. While this perspective is not exhaustive, it aims to highlight the key statutes that frequently come into play in real-world legal practice.

- **Monopoly Regulation And Fair Trade Act (독점규제 및 공정거래에 관한 법률)**

One of my first assignments as a law firm associate was drafting a merger filing. I had no idea what a merger filing was or why it was required—this wasn't something covered in law school. Following the partner's instructions, I reviewed the client's information, used the template, and translated it into Korean for the regulatory submission. Later, I learned that this task was mandated by Article 11 of the MRFTA, with detailed drafting guidelines provided by the Korea Fair Trade Commission (KFTC).

The MRFTA is Korea's primary statute for ensuring fair competition, combining elements of the Sherman Act, Clayton Act, Federal Trade Commission Act, and Hart-Scott-Rodino (HSR) Act in the United States. It regulates dominant companies to prevent unfair market control, requires reporting of major mergers, targets cartels and unfair practices, and restricts conglomerate activities that reduce competition. Corporate counsel and business professionals in Korea regularly rely on this statute to ensure compliance in transactions. The KFTC enforces these rules with significant fines for violations, making a clear understanding of the act important for those involved in corporate legal matters.

「별표1」 ☞ 기재요령 및 첨부서류는 뒷면참조

<table>
<tr><td colspan="7">주식취득(또는 소유)의 신고서</td><td>신고 유형[1]</td><td>□ 일반신고
□ 간이신고</td></tr>
<tr><td rowspan="8">[2] 신고인</td><td rowspan="2">회 사 명
(또는성명)</td><td colspan="2" rowspan="2"></td><td rowspan="2">대표자
성 명</td><td colspan="2">(한글)</td><td>설립일</td><td></td></tr>
<tr><td colspan="2">(한자)</td><td>상장일</td><td></td></tr>
<tr><td>주 소</td><td colspan="3"></td><td rowspan="2">연락처
(대리인)</td><td colspan="4" rowspan="2">담당자 :
전화 :
팩스 :</td></tr>
<tr><td>사업자
번호[3]</td><td colspan="3"></td></tr>
<tr><td rowspan="3">재무상황[4]
(단위:백만원)</td><td>납입자본금</td><td colspan="2"></td><td>자본총계</td><td colspan="3"></td></tr>
<tr><td>경상이익</td><td colspan="2"></td><td>당기순이익</td><td colspan="3"></td></tr>
<tr><td>자산총액
(기업집단전체)</td><td colspan="2">( )</td><td>매 출 액
(기업집단전체)
국내매출액
(기업집단전체)[5]</td><td colspan="3">( )
( )</td></tr>
<tr><td>주요사업</td><td colspan="7"></td></tr>
<tr><td rowspan="9">상대회사</td><td rowspan="2">회사명</td><td colspan="2" rowspan="2"></td><td rowspan="2">대표자
성 명</td><td colspan="2">(한글)</td><td>설립일</td><td></td></tr>
<tr><td colspan="2">(한자)</td><td>상장일</td><td></td></tr>
<tr><td>주 소</td><td colspan="3"></td><td>연락처
(대리인)</td><td colspan="4">담당자 :
전화 :
팩스 :</td></tr>
<tr><td rowspan="3">재무상황[4]
(단위:백만원)</td><td>납입자본금</td><td colspan="2"></td><td>자본총계</td><td colspan="3"></td></tr>
<tr><td>경상이익</td><td colspan="2"></td><td>당기순이익</td><td colspan="3"></td></tr>
<tr><td>자산총액
(기업집단전체)</td><td colspan="2">( )</td><td>매 출 액
(기업집단전체)[5]
국내매출액
(기업집단전체)[5]</td><td colspan="3">( )
( )</td></tr>
<tr><td>주요사업</td><td colspan="7"></td></tr>
<tr><td rowspan="2">소규모
피취득
회사[6]</td><td colspan="2">거래금액[7]</td><td colspan="5"></td></tr>
<tr><td colspan="2">국내활동수준[8]</td><td colspan="5">□ 직전 3년간 국내 시장에서 월 100만 명 이상을 대상으로 상품 또는 용역을 판매 · 제공한 적이 있는 경우
□ 직전 3년간 국내 연구시설 또는 연구 인력을 보유 · 활용해 왔고 국내 연구시설, 연구인력 또는 국내 연구활동 등에 대한 연간 지출액이 300억원 이상인 적이 있는 경우</td></tr>
<tr><td rowspan="6">주식
취득
내용</td><td colspan="3" rowspan="2">주 주</td><td colspan="2">주식 소유비율 (%)</td><td rowspan="2">총취득금액</td><td colspan="2" rowspan="2">취득일(계약일)[11]</td></tr>
<tr><td>취 득 전</td><td>취 득 후</td></tr>
<tr><td rowspan="3">신고인
관련</td><td colspan="2">당해신고인</td><td></td><td></td><td></td><td colspan="2"></td></tr>
<tr><td rowspan="2">특수
관계인</td><td>계열회사[9]</td><td></td><td></td><td></td><td colspan="2"></td></tr>
<tr><td>회사 외의 자[10]</td><td></td><td></td><td></td><td colspan="2"></td></tr>
<tr><td colspan="3">계</td><td></td><td></td><td></td><td colspan="2"></td></tr>
<tr><td colspan="9">「독점규제 및 공정거래에 관한 법률」 제11조(기업결합의 신고) 및 동법시행령 제18조부터 제20조의 규정에 의하여 위와 같이 신고합니다.

20 . . . 신고회사[12] 대표자 (인)

공 정 거 래 위 원 회 귀 중</td></tr>
</table>

Korea merger filing template. (Source: Table 1 of KFTC Guideline for Merger Filings)

▪ Labor Standards Act (근로기준법)

As a practicing lawyer in Korea, regardless of your expertise, you'll often encounter questions about labor issues like wages, leave, and termination—much like a doctor frequently treats sore throats. The Labor Standards Act (LSA) of Korea, enacted in 1953, sets the minimum standards for employment, covering wages, working hours, and leave entitlements. The U.S. equivalent of this law is primarily the Fair Labor Standards Act (FLSA).

One key difference is Korea's strict approach to termination. Unlike the U.S., where "at-will" employment allows termination without cause (except for discriminatory reasons), Korea requires just cause for termination. Violations of the LSA can also result in criminal penalties for employers, which is not typical under U.S. labor laws.

▪ Personal Information Protection Act (개인정보보호법)

When I began my legal career in 2007, personal information protection was a relatively minor concern. Over time, with advancements in technology and the enactment of Korea's Personal Information Protection Act (PIPA), the focus on data privacy has grown significantly. Introduced in 2011 and amended in 2020, PIPA provides a comprehensive framework for data protection that closely aligns with the EU's General Data Protection Regulation (GDPR). It establishes clear requirements for consent in data processing, mandates safeguards for personal information, and requires express consent for direct marketing. Additionally, all organizations, regardless of size, must appoint a data protection officer, emphasizing accountability in managing personal data.

Unlike the United States, which lacks a single, comprehensive privacy law at the federal level and instead relies on a patchwork of sector-specific laws and state-level regulations, Korea's PIPA provides a unified framework for privacy protection. Korea's alignment with international standards has been recognized through its adequacy decision under the EU GDPR, which allows the free transfer of personal data between Korea and the European Economic Area (EEA) without the need for additional safeguards, such as Standard Contractual Clauses (SCCs). Businesses seeking to comply with PIPA can access resources such as the official website privacy.go.kr to assess their practices and ensure alignment with the law's requirements.

- **Unfair Competition Prevention And Trade Secret Protection Act (부정경쟁방지 및 영업비밀보호에 관한 법률) and other IP laws**

As intangible assets like data and technology gain increasing importance, laws such as the Unfair Competition Prevention and Trade Secret Protection Act (UCPA) and the Act on Prevention of Divulgence and Protection of Industrial Technology (산업기술의 유출방지 및 보호에 관한 법률, APDPI) have become central to corporate counsel's work.

The UCPA, first enacted in 1961 and regularly updated, provides the legal framework for protecting trade secrets. It defines trade secrets, outlines what constitutes misappropriation, and criminalizes unauthorized acquisition, disclosure, or use. The APDPI focuses on preventing the leakage of industrial technology to maintain competitiveness. Violations of trade secrets or industrial technology laws can result in civil injunctions, damages, and criminal penalties, including up to 10 years' imprisonment or fines of up to 500 million KRW, with harsher penalties for overseas leakage. Additionally, the Patent Act (특허법), Trademark Act (상표법), Design Protection Act (디자인보호법), and Copyright Act (저작권법) govern different aspects of intellectual property. These laws cover patents for inventions, trademarks for branding, designs for product aesthetics, and copyrights for creative works. For legal professionals, the Trade Secret Protection Center (https://www.tradesecret.or.kr), operated by the Korea Patent Office, offers resources such as templates and educational materials to help with trade secret management.

- **Financial Investment Services And Capital Markets Act (자본시장과 금융투자업에 관한 법률)**

The Financial Investment Services and Capital Markets Act (FISCMA) did not exist when I was in law school. Established on August 3, 2007, FISCMA consolidated regulations that were previously scattered across six different laws. It introduced a principle-based framework, defining only what is prohibited, allowing flexibility and fostering financial innovation while maintaining market integrity. The Act centralizes licensing for financial investment businesses, outlines service provider responsibilities, and regulates capital market operations, including insider trading.

FISCMA's comprehensive scope is similar to what is covered in the U.S. by multiple laws, including the Securities Act of 1933, the Securities Exchange Act of 1934, the Dodd-Frank Act, and the Sarbanes-Oxley Act. FISCMA addresses investor protection, market regulation, and financial services oversight under a unified framework.

A key focus of FISCMA is investor protection. Today, individuals investing in financial products face a more rigorous process involving detailed disclosures and paperwork, designed to ensure they are well-informed. Additionally, the Act reflects modern ESG trends, such as a recent amendment requiring large companies to appoint at least one female outside director, integrating ethical considerations into corporate governance. For listed companies, FISCMA supplements the Civil and Commercial Acts, making it a priority for regulatory compliance.

▪ Tax and Currency related Laws

I must admit, my expertise in this area is limited. Even experienced attorneys at top law firms often find tax, customs, and currency matters challenging unless they specialize in them. In corporations, these areas are typically managed by the finance department rather than legal. However, as a corporate general counsel, it's important to have broad awareness—much like a school nurse who may not diagnose every issue but knows when to call in a specialist.

The Corporate Tax Act (법인세법), Value Added Tax Act (부가가치세법), and **Income Tax Act (소득세법)** are essential for understanding corporate and individual taxation, as they directly affect business operations and strategic planning. Foreign entities, in particular, should familiarize themselves with these laws and the country's tax treaties to ensure compliance and gain strategic advantages. The **Foreign Exchange Act (외국환거래법)** governs currency exchange, crucial for international business, and is supported by the **Foreign Investment Promotion Law (외국인투자촉진법)**, which offers incentives such as tax credits and simplified fund remittance for foreign investors. The **National Tax Service (NTS)** and the **Bank of Korea**, along with designated foreign exchange banks, play key roles in managing these processes. The NTS, similar to the U.S. **Internal Revenue Service (IRS)**, oversees tax collection and enforcement, providing resources to help both corporate and individual taxpayers comply efficiently with tax regulations.

In summary, the statutes we've covered are fundamental to legal practice in Korea, particularly for corporate lawyers and inhouse counsels. However, understanding these statutes alone is not sufficient. Their full application requires careful consideration of the subordinate rules and regulations that complement and enforce them. In the next section, we will explore the broader legislative structure, focusing on the detailed regulations that give life to these statutes and guide their practical implementation.

Bullet Point Summary

- **Expansive Statutes**: Korea's legal framework contains 1,825 laws, ranging from broad legal codes to highly specialized statutes, highlighting the depth and detail of the system.

- **Core Statutes for Legal Education**: Foundational statutes like the Civil Act, Commercial Act, and Criminal Act, tested in the Bar Exam, serve as essential frameworks for understanding Korean law, though their practical application may be limited.

- **Real Core Statutes in Practice**: Lawyers focus on industry-specific laws aligned with their roles. Corporate lawyers frequently deal with the Monopoly Regulation and Fair Trade Act, Labor Standards Act, and Personal Information Protection Act to address fair competition, labor compliance, and data protection. They also rely on the Unfair Competition Prevention and Trade Secret Protection Act and other IP laws to safeguard intangible assets. In finance, the Financial Investment Services and Capital Markets Act governs investor protection and financial transactions. Additionally, tax and currency-related laws, though often managed by finance teams, require legal oversight to ensure compliance and strategic alignment.

SECTION 3. THE LEGISLATIVE STRUCTURE

NOW THAT WE'VE REVIEWED Korea's major statutes (법률), it's essential to understand the broader legislative structure that brings these laws into practical effect. Statutes like the Minimum Wage Act (최저임금법) provide the legal framework, but the specifics—such as the actual wage level—are set through subordinate regulations like Public Notices (고시). This highlights the need to go beyond statutes to fully grasp how the law functions in practice. In this section, we will explore how statutes are applied and expanded through lower-tier regulations.

THE HIERARCHICAL STRUCTURE

At the heart of Korea's legal system are Statutes or Acts (법률), comparable to the United States Code (U.S.C.) in the U.S. These Acts, established by the National Assembly—Korea's principal legislative body, similar to the U.S. Congress—set the core legal frameworks. However, understanding how these statutes operate requires examining subordinate regulations, namely **Enforcement Decrees (시행령)** and **Enforcement Rules (시행규칙)**, which are akin to the Code of Federal Regulations (CFR) in the U.S.

- **Enforcement Decrees**, issued by the President and deliberated by the State Council, offer detailed guidance on how laws are applied to ensure their effective operation.

- **Enforcement Rules**, established by ministries and agencies, address specific enforcement details, providing clear instructions for compliance.

- **Public Notices (고시)** and **Guidance (지침)** function similarly to administrative rulings in the U.S., containing precise details for day-to-day application and adaptation to changing circumstances.

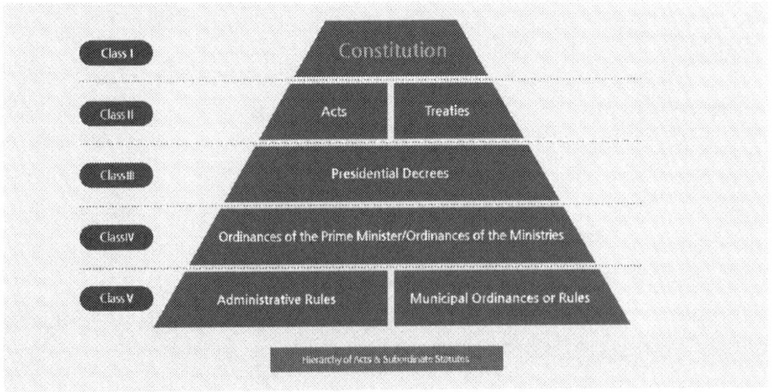

(Source: https://elaw.klri.re.kr/eng_service/struct.do)

REAL LIFE APPLICATIONS

A practical example of this structure is the **Minimum Wage Act**. The Act itself establishes the framework for setting the minimum wage, but it does not specify the amount. Article 8(1) mandates the Minister of Employment and Labor to determine the minimum wage annually by August 5th, with Article 10(2) requiring prompt public notification. However, the actual figure, such as the 2024 minimum wage of KRW 9,860 per hour, is communicated through a Public Notice issued by the Minister of Employment and Labor. This demonstrates how substantive details guiding practical application are often found in subordinate regulations.

「최저임금법」 제10조제1항에 따라 2024년 1월 1일부터 2024년 12월 31일까지 적용되는 최저임금액을 다음과 같이 고시합니다.

2023. 8. 4.

고 용 노 동 부 장 관

1. 최저임금액

결정단위 / 업 종	시 간 급
모 든 산 업	**9,860원**

◈ **월 환산액 2,060,740원**: 주 소정근로 40시간을 근무할 경우, 월 환산 기준시간 수 209시간(주당 유급주휴 8시간 포함) 기준

2. 최저임금의 사업의 종류별 구분 여부

○ 사업의 종류별 구분 없이 모든 사업장에 동일하게 적용

3. 최저임금 적용 기간: 2024. 1. 1. ~ 2024. 12. 31.

Another example is the **Improper Solicitation and Graft Act (부정청탁및금품등수수의금지에관한법률)**, often referred as the **Kim Young-Ran Act**. Commonly understood that gifts up to KRW 50,000 (approximately USD 38) are allowed to public officials, this specific threshold is not detailed in the Act itself. Instead, Article 8 broadly prohibits the receipt of money or gifts but allows exceptions, such as 'Money, goods, etc., the value of which is within the limits prescribed by Presidential Decree, in the form of food and beverages, congratulatory or condolence money, gifts, etc., offered for purposes of facilitating performance of duties, social relationships, rituals, or aid.' The exact permissible amounts are listed under Schedule 1 of Article 17, which outlines these exceptions, such as for meals, condolences, and congratulatory gifts.

<u>음식물 · 경조사비 · 선물 등의 가액 범위</u>(제17조제1항 관련)

1. 음식물(제공자와 공직자등이 함께 하는 식사, 다과, 주류, 음료, 그 밖에 이에 준하는 것을 말한다): 3만원
2. 경조사비: 축의금 · 조의금은 5만원. 다만, 축의금 · 조의금을 대신하는 화환 · 조화는 10만원으로 한다.
3. 선물: 다음 각 목의 금품등을 제외한 일체의 물품, 상품권(물품상품권 및 용역상품권만 해당하며, 이하 "상품권"이라 한다) 및 그 밖에 이에 준하는 것은 5만원.

These examples illustrate how statutes form the backbone of legal regulation, while lower-tier regulations provide the flexibility needed to adapt to evolving social and economic conditions. Subordinate rules bridge the gap between general legislative principles and practical application, ensuring the legal system remains responsive and effective. For a deeper understanding, legal professionals should consult relevant ministries and government committees. These platforms provide access to the full range of Acts, Enforcement Decrees, Enforcement Rules, and Public Notices, offering a comprehensive view of both overarching principles and detailed regulatory applications.

Bullet Point Summary

- **Layered Legislative Framework**: Korean statutes are supplemented by Enforcement Decrees, Enforcement Rules, and Public Notices to ensure detailed and practical application of laws.
- **Examples of Practical Application:** The Minimum Wage Act and Kim Young-Ran Act illustrate how statutes provide frameworks, while subordinate regulations set specific rules.
- **Resources for Legal Practice**: Access to ministry and government platforms is essential for legal professionals to stay informed on both high-level principles and detailed regulations.

CHAPTER 2.
THE JUDICIAL SYSTEM

A solid understanding of the Korean judicial system is essential for advising clients, even for in-house counsel who rarely engage in litigation. Familiarity with key legal terms is the first step. This chapter provides an overview of the core components, clarifying their roles within the legal framework. We will explore the structure and functions of courts and prosecutors' offices, the civil litigation process, criminal investigations and trials, and major government institutions influencing corporate matters. By focusing on the most relevant 20% of the system, this chapter aims to equip you with the knowledge that will cover 80% of your practical needs.

SECTION 1: COURT AND PROSECUTORS' OFFICES

THE COURT STRUCTURE

THE KOREAN JUDICIAL system operates under a unified structure, differing from the dual federal-state system in the U.S. At its core are the general courts: the Supreme Court, the High Courts, and the District Courts. Together, they form the backbone of Korea's judiciary, ensuring comprehensive legal adjudication.

▪ The Supreme Court (대법원)

At the top of the judicial hierarchy is the Supreme Court, Korea's final appellate authority, akin to the U.S. Supreme Court. It resolves cases that have progressed through lower courts. While the overall number of court cases in Korea has decreased over the past decade (from 18 million in 2013 to 16 million in 2022), cases reaching the Supreme Court have surged (from 36,000 in 2013 to 52,000 in 2022). Each of the 12 justices handles an annual caseload of approximately 4,000 cases, reflecting the court's efficiency and the heavy responsibilities placed on its justices.

▪ The High Courts (고등법원)

The High Courts serve as regional appellate courts, reviewing appeals from District Courts to ensure consistency in the application of law. They play a role similar to the U.S. Courts of Appeals, functioning as intermediaries between trial courts and the Supreme Court.

▪ The District Courts (지방법원)

District Courts sit at the foundation of Korea's judicial system. As of 2024, 18 District Courts are strategically located across the nation to ensure access to justice. These courts handle the majority of civil and criminal cases, serving as the primary trial courts. They correspond to U.S. District Courts and are central to the day-to-day administration of justice.

▪ Specialized Courts

In addition to general courts, Korea's judiciary includes specialized courts, such as the Patent Court, Family Court, Rehabilitation Court, and Administrative Court (특허, 가정, 회생, 행정법원). These courts cater to specific legal domains, functioning like subject matter experts within the judiciary. For example, Family Courts handle domestic and familial disputes, such as divorces, adoptions, and child custody cases, similar to state-level family courts in the U.S. Administrative Courts ensure the legality of government actions and regulations, similar to how U.S. federal courts handle administrative law disputes.

(Source: https://www.scourt.go.kr/region/organization/regionOrgan.jsp)

Legal proceedings within Korean courts follow a structured path. Trials are presided over by a single judge or a panel of three. Although proceedings are generally open to the public, exceptions exist for cases involving national security or public order. Even in such instances, final judgments remain accessible to the public. If dissatisfied with a first-instance judgment, parties can appeal. Most appeals are heard by the High Courts, but cases tried by a single judge may be appealed to local District Courts' appellate branches. The Supreme Court handles further appeals, functioning as the ultimate judicial authority.

Practical Tips

- Identifying the Appropriate Court: Use the official Supreme Court of Korea's tool to find the correct court for filing your case. Access the tool here (https://www.scourt.go.kr/region/location/RegionSearchListAction.work)
- Researching Court Rulings: The Supreme Court offers a comprehensive database of rulings. Explore the database here(https://glaw.scourt.go.kr/wsjo/panre/sjo050.do#1710917037922)
- English Translations of Rulings: The Court Library provides access to English translations of selected court decisions. Browse available translations here (https://library.scourt.go.kr/search/judg/case/eng)

THE PROSECUTORS' OFFICE STRUCTURE

The prosecutorial system in Korea is distinctively centralized, a stark contrast to the U.S. model. Under the Ministry of Justice, which operates under the direct influence of the President, Korean prosecutors are endowed with a broader scope of investigative powers. Unlike their American counterparts, where investigative duties predominantly fall to the police, Korean prosecutors lead both the prosecution of cases and criminal investigations. Recently, amendments have aimed to reduce prosecutors' investigative powers, shifting some responsibilities to other agencies. Despite these changes, prosecutors in Korea still hold significant power, especially in leading criminal investigations and prosecutions.

The structure of the prosecutorial offices parallels the hierarchy of the judiciary, creating a coherent alignment across different levels.

The system is divided into three tiers: the Supreme Prosecutors' Office (대검찰청), High Prosecutors' Offices (고등검찰청), and District Prosecutors' Offices (지방검찰청). This mirrors the judicial structure—Supreme Court, High Courts, and District Courts—enabling smooth coordination between investigative and judicial processes. There is 1 Supreme Prosecutors' Office, 6 High Prosecutors' Offices, 18 District Prosecutors' Offices, and 42 branch prosecutors' offices, ensuring comprehensive coverage across the nation.

Organization of the Prosecutors' Offices

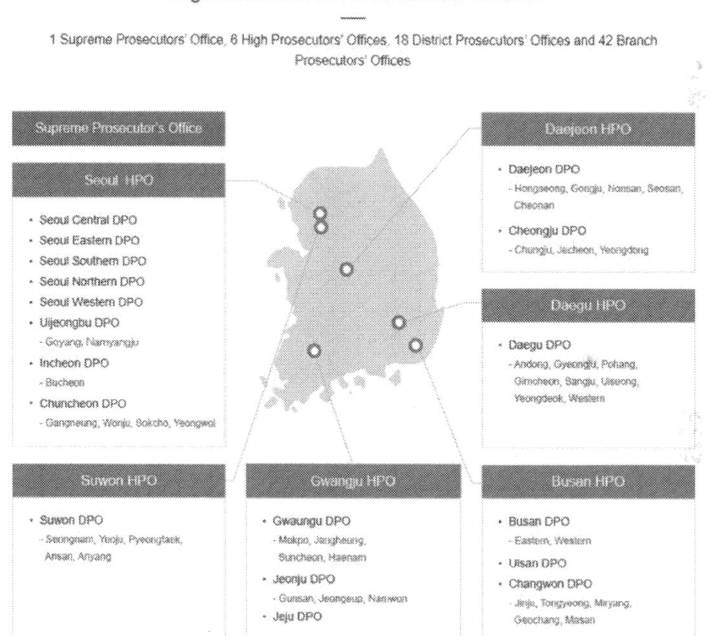

A defining feature of Korea's prosecutorial framework is the principle of unity among prosecutors, known as Principle of Prosecutorial Unit(검사동일체원칙). Article 7 of the Prosecution Office Act mandates that prosecutors follow the directives and supervision of their superior officers, reinforcing centralized command and operational cohesion.

The language governing prosecutors' obedience has evolved over time. Previously, the law stated that "prosecutors shall obey orders from superiors in prosecutorial affairs". In 2004, this was moderated to "prosecutors must adhere to the directives and supervision of their superior officers." This change, while subtle, reflects a shift towards a more collaborative tone while maintaining the expectation of unity and obedience within the prosecutorial ranks. However, the core principle of hierarchical obedience remains embedded in the legal culture, emphasizing unity while accommodating a more modern approach to leadership and teamwork.

Bullet Point Summary

- **Unified Judicial System**: Korea's court system is centralized, with the Supreme Court, High Courts, and District Courts forming the core. Specialized courts, such as the Patent and Administrative Courts, handle specific legal areas.

- **Centralized Prosecutorial System**: The prosecutorial structure mirrors the judicial hierarchy, with the Supreme Prosecutors' Office at the top, followed by High and District Prosecutors' Offices, ensuring nationwide coverage and coordination.

- **Principle of Prosecutorial Unity**: Under the Prosecution Office Act, prosecutors operate under a hierarchical structure, adhering to directives from superiors, reflecting the "Principle of Prosecutorial Unity". While recent amendments have softened the language from “obeying orders” to “adhering to directives,” the centralized nature of the system remains intact.

SECTION 2: CIVIL LITIGATION PROCEDURE

TYPES OF CIVIL CASES BASED ON CLAIM AMOUNT

BEFORE EXAMINING THE civil litigation procedure, it is essential to understand how claim amounts (소가) determine case types and jurisdiction.

1. Small Claims (소액사건): For claims up to 30 million won (approximately USD 23,100 as of July 2024). These cases follow an expedited process with a single judge issuing swift decisions, often without providing detailed written grounds for the ruling.

2. Single-Judge Hearing (민사단독): Applicable to claims between 30 million and 200 million won (approximately USD 23,100 to USD 154,000). A single judge presides over these cases.

3. Panel Hearing (민사합의): For claims exceeding 200 million won (over USD 154,000). These cases are heard by a three-judge panel.

The claim amount determines both the trial process and the appellate route. Panel hearing cases are heard at the District Court and then appealed to the High Court. Small claims and single-judge hearing cases are appealed to the District Court, with all third-instance appeals proceeding to the Supreme Court.

CIVIL LITIGATION PROCEDURE

Civil litigation begins when the plaintiff files a complaint (소장) with a local District Court. To ensure the correct venue, plaintiffs can use the official Korean Court Locations website (https://www.scourt.go.kr/region/location/RegionSearchListAction.work).Korean courts also allow electronic filing through the Electronic Case Filing System (민사전자소송제도), which has significantly streamlined the litigation process since its introduction in 2011. Plaintiffs initiate proceedings by agreeing to the electronic litigation procedure and submitting claims with electronic signatures. Defendants, upon receiving the claim by mail, use the provided authentication number and case number to submit responses online.

Once filed, the court serves a copy of the complaint to the defendant to notify them of the proceedings (송달). The defendant must submit a written response (답변서) within 30 days from receipt, addressing the plaintiff's allegations.

Following this, both parties engage in trial preparation by submitting written arguments (준비서면) to organize their positions. The court holds hearings (변론기일) to examine the arguments and evidence presented by both sides. After the hearings, the court renders a judgment (판결선고).

If either party is dissatisfied with the ruling, they may appeal (항소) within two weeks. A final appeal to the Supreme Court (대법원) is available for legal review (상고). The trial process focuses on fact-finding in the first and second instances, while the Supreme Court primarily reviews legal interpretations. However, the Supreme Court rarely overturns lower court decisions and often employs the Summary Dismissal of Unfit Cases process (심리불속행 기각) to efficiently manage its caseload, dismissing 70-80% of appeals within four months.

While the official litigation process starts with filing a complaint, lawyers often recommend using content-certified mail (내용증명) as a strategic pre-litigation step. The post office certifies that a document with specified content was sent to the intended recipient at a specific time. It should be noted that this certification does not confirm the accuracy or truthfulness of the content; it merely verifies that a document with specified content was delivered to the recipient at a specific time. Although not part of the formal litigation process, it demonstrates seriousness and intent, potentially encouraging resolution without court intervention. Although there is no standardized form for content-certified mail, various websites offer templates that can be tailored to specific situations.

Bullet Point Summary

- **Types of Cases by Claim Amount**: Small claims (under 30 million won) are handled swiftly by a single judge, mid-range cases (30-200 million won) use single-judge hearings, and larger claims (above 200 million won) require a three-judge panel.

- **Civil Litigation Process**: The process includes filing a complaint, submitting responses, preparing for hearings, attending hearings, and appealing to decisions if necessary. Appeals are typically limited, with many cases dismissed summarily by the Supreme Court.

- **Electronic Filing and Pre-Litigation Strategy**: The Electronic Case Filing System simplifies the process for plaintiffs and defendants, while content-certified mail offers a way to demonstrate intent and potentially resolve disputes before formal proceedings.

SECTION 3: CRIMINAL INVESTIGATION AND LITIGATION PROCEDURE

OVERVIEW

THE CRIMINAL JUSTICE process in Korea follows a structured path, beginning with police investigations, moving through prosecutorial review, and concluding with a court trial. Each phase ensures thorough investigation and fair judgment, with distinct roles assigned to police, prosecutors, and judges. The process typically starts when the police receive or recognize a crime report. If the police gather sufficient evidence, they forward the case to the prosecutor. The prosecutor then decides whether to press charges, and if so, the case proceeds to court for the final determination of guilt or innocence.

INVESTIGATION

When an investigation is initiated, the prosecutor or investigative agency leads the process, with measures divided into non-compulsory and compulsory categories. Non-compulsory measures include requesting documents, conducting inquiries, interviewing individuals, and seeking expert opinions. These actions are crucial for gathering information and building a case, but they do not impose any direct restrictions on the suspect's freedom or property. In contrast, compulsory measures—such as arrest, detention, and search and seizure—have a more significant impact, as they directly affect personal liberties and property rights. Due to their seriousness, the Korean Constitution mandates that these measures require a judicial warrant, which only prosecutors can request. Police officers, therefore, cannot directly apply for a warrant and must collaborate with prosecutors to proceed with such actions, underscoring the importance of judicial oversight in safeguarding individual rights.

If the evidence gathered during the investigation is deemed insufficient, the prosecutor may request further investigation from the police. However, if the prosecutor determines that prosecution is not justified—whether due to a lack of evidence, the absence of a crime, or jurisdictional issues—they may decide not to press charges. In these cases, the complainant has the right to appeal the non-prosecution decision within 30 days. Additionally, if key witnesses or the suspect are unavailable, the prosecutor may choose to suspend prosecution temporarily, even if sufficient evidence exists to move forward.

CRIMINAL TRIAL

Once the prosecutor files charges, the case moves into the court system, and the suspect is now referred to as a defendant. Several types of trials exist to ensure a tailored and fair examination of each case.

▪ Regular Trial

The regular trial process begins with a **pre-trial phase**, where the court serves the defendant with written information detailing the charges. The defendant submits a written opinion in response, and both sides exchange relevant evidence, much like the exchange of documents in civil litigation. If necessary, the defendant can request access to the prosecutor's documents and witnesses for better preparation.

Once the pre-trial proceedings are complete, the trial itself begins. It starts with notifying the defendant of their rights, confirming their identity, and thoroughly examining the evidence. If the defendant denies the charges, the court conducts a detailed examination to ensure every aspect is scrutinized. However, if the defendant admits guilt, the case may proceed through a **simplified trial process (간이공판절차)**, as outlined in Article 286-2 of the Criminal Procedure Act. This approach allows the court to adopt a more streamlined procedure, bypassing some of the formalities of a regular trial. The trial concludes with final arguments from the prosecutor, defense counsel, and the defendant. After all arguments are presented, the judge delivers a verdict.

▪ Brief Procedure (약식절차)

For certain cases, particularly when seeking punishment by fine, the prosecutor may opt for a brief procedure under Article 448 of the Criminal Procedure Act. In this process, the court reviews the case based solely on documents and issues a decision without holding a formal oral trial. If the court deems the case inappropriate for a brief procedure, it will refer the case to a regular trial. Both the defendant and the prosecutor have the right to request a regular trial within seven days of receiving the decision. If no request is made, the brief procedure's decision becomes final and carries the same legal weight as a regular judgment.

▪ Summary Judgment (즉결심판)

The summary judgment process, regulated by the Summary Trial Act (즉결심판에 관한 절차법), addresses minor offenses efficiently. After the police file a complaint, a district court judge reviews the case and delivers a swift ruling. As with the brief procedure, either party may request a regular trial within seven days of the decision. If no request is made, the summary judgment stands as final.

DISTINCTIONS FROM THE U.S. SYSTEM

Korea's criminal justice system differs significantly from the U.S. system in several key aspects. While the U.S. employs an adversarial system where the prosecution and defense present evidence to an impartial jury, Korea follows a more inquisitorial approach. In this system, judges play a proactive role in gathering and evaluating evidence, taking on investigative functions that are less common for their U.S. counterparts.

In the U.S., defendants often negotiate for a lesser sentence in exchange for a guilty plea. Korea, however, employs a system known as "recommendation for leniency," where prosecutors can suggest reduced sentences in return for the defendant's cooperation and confession. This allows prosecutors to suggest a reduced sentence in exchange for the defendant's cooperation and confession, but it lacks the formal structure typically seen in U.S. plea bargaining.

Finally, although jury trials do exist in Korea, they are not constitutional rights as they are in some other legal systems. Instead, the right to a jury trial in Korea is statutory, meaning defendants may request them, but they are not guaranteed in every case. Additionally, even when a jury is involved, its verdict serves as an advisory opinion, leaving the judge with the final authority to determine the outcome.

Bullet Point Summary

- **Criminal Investigation**: Korean prosecutors play a central role in investigations and pressing charges, with police collaborating closely under prosecutorial oversight. Judicial warrants are required for compulsory measures like arrests or searches.
- **Criminal Trial Types**: Trials range from regular trials to expedited processes like brief procedures and summary judgments, ensuring proportional handling of cases. Defendants may request regular trials if dissatisfied with summary procedures.
- **Comparison to U.S. System**: Korea's inquisitorial approach involves judges in fact-finding, with limited plea bargaining options and non-binding jury verdicts, distinguishing it from the adversarial U.S. system.

SECTION 4: MAJOR GOVERNMENT ORGANIZATIONS

IN CORPORATE LAW, understanding the role and influence of key government organizations is essential. While the legislative branch makes laws and the judicial branch, through courts and prosecutors, interprets and enforces them, the executive branch is where much of the day-to-day corporate legal work occurs. Legal education often focuses on statutes and case law, but in practice, much of corporate legal work revolves around how government organizations implement and enforce these laws. Although not formally part of the judicial system, many government organizations function as quasi-judicial bodies, making decisions that directly affect businesses. In fact, their policies and enforcement actions often shape corporate operations more directly than court decisions.

This section offers an overview of South Korea's executive branch and introduces the major government bodies that regulate and oversee corporate activities.

THE EXECUTIVE BRANCH OVERVIEW

The executive branch of the South Korean government comprises a structured network of administrative bodies responsible for executing the state's affairs. While "government organization" can broadly encompass legislative and judicial institutions, it generally refers to the administrative framework of the executive branch.

At the top of the executive branch is the President (대통령), who serves as the chief of state. Below the President is the Prime Minister (국무총리), acting on the President's behalf to direct and supervise the heads of central administrative agencies. The Prime Minister also oversees three key ministries: the Ministry of Personnel Management (인사혁신처, MPM), the Ministry of Government Legislation (법제처, MOLEG), and the Ministry of Food and Drug Safety (식품의약품안전처, MFDS). Additionally, the Prime Minister manages five commissions, including the Korea Fair Trade Commission (공정거래위원회, KFTC), Financial Services Commission (금융위원회, FSC), Anti-Corruption and Civil Rights Commission (국민권익위원회, ACRC), Personal Information Protection Commission (개인정보보호위원회, PIPC), and the Nuclear Safety and Security Commission (원자력안전위원회, NSSC).

Directly reporting to the President are 19 ministries, such as the Ministry of Economy and Finance (기획재정부, MOEF), Ministry of Justice (법무부, MOJ), Ministry of Trade, Industry and Energy (산업통상자원부, MOTIE), Ministry of Employment and Labor (고용노동부, MOEL), and the Ministry of SMEs and Startups (중소벤처기업부, MSS). Each ministry manages specialized agencies, including the National Tax Service (국세청, NTS), Korea Customs Service (관세청, KCS), Supreme Prosecutors' Office (대검찰청, SPO), National Police Agency (경찰청, NPA), Korean Intellectual Property Office (특허청, KIPO), and the Korea Disease Control and Prevention Agency (질병관리청, KDCA).

The official government organizational chart, updated as of May 27, 2024, is available in English.

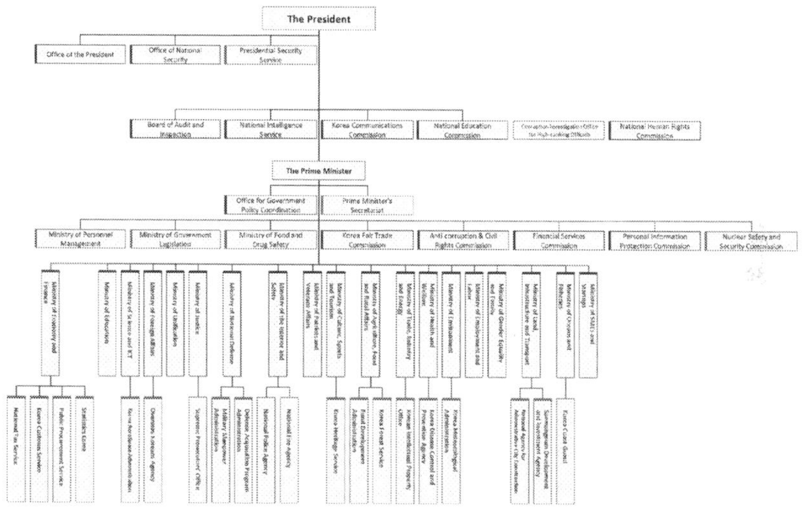

(Source: https://www.org.go.kr/orgnzt/chart/viewEng.do)

This complex structure ensures that laws and regulations are enforced across multiple sectors, directly influencing how businesses operate. For corporate legal counsel, certain agencies are more frequently encountered. For example, the Korea Fair Trade Commission (공정거래위원회, KFTC) is relevant when ensuring contracts in sales or marketing comply with fair business practice regulations. The Financial Services Commission (금융위원회, FSC), along with the Financial Supervisory Service (금융감독원, FSS), is engaged in major corporate transaction and disclosures, often in collaboration with the finance department. Employment disputes, handled by HR, typically involve the Ministry of Employment and Labor (고용노동부, MOEL). Additionally, the Korean Intellectual Property Office (특허청, KIPO) and the National Tax Service (국세청,

NTS) are essential for intellectual property and tax compliance matters.

In the following section, I will provide an in-depth examination of these key organizations, outlining their roles, regulatory authority, and impact on corporate legal practice.

UNDERSTANDING THE MAJOR PLAYERS

For litigation attorneys, the primary stakeholders are judges and prosecutors. However, for in-house counsels, key stakeholders—often referred to as "gap" (갑) in Korean—are government agencies that directly impact business operations. The term "gap" comes from "gap-eul" (갑을관계), a term used to describe a power dynamic in which the party in the "gap" position holds more authority or influence. In the corporate world, these government organizations regulate critical areas such as contract terms, corporate transactions, finance, employment, intellectual property, and taxation. Understanding when and how they intersect with your company's activities is crucial for maintaining compliance and managing risk effectively.

Let's start with the Korea Fair Trade Commission (KFTC, 공정거래위원회).

- **Korea Fair Trade Commission (KFTC, 공정거래위원회)**

The Korea Fair Trade Commission (KFTC), one of five commissions under the Prime Minister's office, promotes competition and regulates unfair practices. Similar to the U.S. Federal Trade Commission (FTC), the KFTC's main tasks are to promote competition, protect consumers, and uphold fair business practices. It regulates monopolies, cartels, and other unfair trade practices. However, unlike in the U.S., where antitrust matters are divided between the FTC and the Department of Justice's Antitrust Division, the KFTC is almost solely responsible for all competition and antitrust issues in

South Korea—there is no antitrust division under the Ministry of Justice. Although this structure allows the KFTC's policies and stances to be more directly influenced by the current administration, it also gives the KFTC a more comprehensive role and leads to streamlined, efficient processing. For example, companies only deal with one agency for merger filings, avoiding confusion common in other jurisdictions. For corporate legal counsels, the KFTC is a vital reference point for ensuring business practices remain within legal boundaries.

Mergers and acquisitions are one area where legal counsels frequently rely on KFTC guidelines. The KFTC reviews these transactions to ensure they do not reduce market competition. Legal counsels assess whether a transaction meets the filing threshold, prepare filings in compliance with KFTC requirements, and anticipate any potential competition law issues.

The KFTC's role in consumer protection is another significant area for legal review. The commission addresses unfair contract terms and monitors advertising to prevent misleading claims. In-house counsel should review contracts, terms of service, and marketing materials to ensure they align with KFTC guidelines. This is especially important in industries like retail and e-commerce, where consumer disputes often arise from unfair practices.

For large corporations working with smaller subcontractors or partners, the KFTC enforces regulations to protect small and medium-sized enterprises (SMEs) from exploitation by dominant companies. Legal counsels review contracts and business practices to ensure fair dealings, especially in areas such as subcontracting, franchising, and large-scale retail.

The KFTC also plays a major role in regulating internal transactions within large conglomerates to limit economic concentration. While there is some debate over whether this is the right approach, authorities often rely on the "undue support" clause of the Monopoly Regulation and Fair Trade Act (MRFTA) to address corporate governance issues in chaebols.

Responding to KFTC investigations, including on-site inspections or dawn raids, is another focus for corporate legal counsels. Much like fire drills, companies must be prepared for these sudden inspections, follow-up information requests, or interviews. The KFTC's Investigation Procedure Rules outline several safeguards designed to protect the rights of the investigated company. For example, before beginning an on-site investigation, officials must present identification and provide a formal investigation document to company employees, explaining the details of the investigation and the company's rights. Legal teams are also allowed to participate throughout the investigation process; if requested, a company's chosen legal representative, including in-house counsel, must be permitted to be present for the entire investigation. Additionally, the rules prohibit investigators from targeting the company's legal or compliance departments, ensuring these departments are not subject to undue scrutiny.

The KFTC's influence spans various sectors of corporate activity. For corporate in-house counsels, KFTC guidelines and contract templates are essential tools for ensuring that corporate practices, contracts, and strategies remain legal and compliant.

▪ Financial Services Commission (FSC, 금융위원회)

The Financial Services Commission (FSC) is one of the five commissions under the Prime Minister's office and serves as the primary authority for financial regulation. It oversees all domestic financial institutions, including banks, insurance companies, and public financial organizations. In addition to supervising the Financial Supervisory Service (FSS), which is explained further below, the FSC sets the overall direction of the financial industry through policymaking, making it the regulatory backbone of Korea's financial sector. It is similar to the U.S. Securities and Exchange Commission (SEC) in terms of regulatory responsibilities for securities markets; however, the FSC's role is broader, and it operates more directly under government oversight.

The FSC is organized into several key bureaus, each responsible for different areas of the financial market. The Financial Consumer Bureau protects consumers, resolves disputes, and ensures that financial products are developed with consumer safety in mind. The Financial Policy Bureau designs financial strategies, analyzes market trends, and creates policies that support SMEs, corporate financing, and Korea's status as a global financial hub. The Financial Industry Bureau regulates banking, insurance, and foreign banks operating in Korea, while the Capital Markets Bureau oversees securities, derivatives, and corporate accounting systems.

Many people often confuse the FSC with the **Financial Supervisory Service (FSS, 금융감독원)** due to their interconnected roles. While the FSC is responsible for policy-making and setting regulatory frameworks, the FSS acts as the operational arm, ensuring institutions comply with these regulations. The FSS monitors financial institutions, investigates misconduct, protects consumers, and resolves disputes. Essentially, the FSC sets the "rules of the game," and the FSS ensures that those rules are followed. The FSC's role is comparable to a blend of the U.S. Securities and Exchange Commission (SEC) and certain roles of the Federal Reserve, while the FSS is similar to the enforcement division of the SEC and the supervisory functions of U.S. financial regulators.

For legal counsels, especially the financial sector, the FSC and FSS are key players you will frequently engage with. In matters like licensing for new financial institutions, you would work closely with the FSC to navigate the approval process. Ongoing compliance for existing financial institutions requires a deep understanding of both FSC and FSS regulations on capital adequacy, risk management, and consumer protection. Additionally, when handling mergers and acquisitions, financial authorities may be involved due to their mission to protect investors, such as strengthened disclosure or filing requirements for the merger process. Cross-border financial transactions are another area where FSC guidelines on foreign exchange and international financial services come into play. Furthermore, in cases of consumer disputes, the FSS plays a pivotal role through its mediation processes. Its guidelines on consumer protection would likely shape the legal advice when handling these issues.

One useful tip for legal counsel is leveraging **DART** (Data Analysis, Retrieval and Transfer System), which is the Korea equivalent of EDGAR (Electronic Data Gathering, Analysis and Retrieval). Operated by the FSS, DART (dart.fss.or.kr) allows companies to file regulatory disclosures online, offering immediate access to corporate and financial information. It's particularly helpful for conducting due diligence, ensuring regulatory compliance, and advising on corporate governance matters.

▪ **Ministry of Employment and Labor (MOEL, 고용노동부)**

The Ministry of Employment and Labor (MOEL) is a cabinet-level ministry responsible for labor policies, employment matters, and workforce development. It combines several functions that, in the U.S. system, are handled by multiple agencies, making it a highly centralized authority. Unlike the U.S. Department of Labor (DOL), which divides responsibilities between agencies like the Occupational Safety and Health Administration (OSHA), the National Labor Relations Board (NLRB), and the Equal Employment Opportunity Commission (EEOC), MOEL integrates these roles under one umbrella.

MOEL enforces labor regulations through laws such as the Labor Standards Act, the Minimum Wage Act, the Occupational Safety and Health Act, and the Serious Accidents Punishment Act. It oversees protections for non-regular workers, including those covered by the

Act on the Protection of Fixed-Term and Part-Time Workers and the Act on the Protection of Temporary Agency Workers. MOEL plays a significant role in promoting gender equality by enforcing the Act on Equal Employment and Support for Work-Family Reconciliation, which mandates gender equality in hiring and workplace policies. The ministry is also at the forefront of addressing workplace harassment, which ties into broader ESG considerations and a company's reputational risk.

Korea's labor dispute resolution system, managed by the Labor Relations Commission (LC), is both distinct and efficient. Initially designed for collective disputes, it also handles individual cases like unfair dismissal claims. Employees can file complaints with the regional LC and escalate them to the national LC or administrative courts if dissatisfied. The LC, housed under MOEL, contrasts with the U.S. model, where the National Labor Relations Board (NLRB) functions as an independent agency.

MOEL provides a wealth of online resources that are particularly useful for legal counsels. Its website offers standardized templates for employment contracts, rules of employment, and detailed guidance on compliance with labor laws. Legal counsels can also access wage calculators and other practical tools that simplify meeting regulatory requirements. These resources streamline the drafting process and ensure companies adhere to Korean labor standards, making MOEL's digital platform an essential resource for navigating employment-related legal issues.

▪ Korean Intellectual Property Office (KIPO, 특허청)

The Korean Intellectual Property Office (KIPO) is the Korean equivalent of the U.S. Patent and Trademark Office. Although it operates under the Ministry of Trade, Industry, and Energy, KIPO functions as an independent office due to its role in managing patents, utility models, designs, and trademarks. This arrangement mirrors the independence of the Prosecutor's Office under the Ministry of Justice.

KIPO oversees the examination, registration, and trial of intellectual property (IP) rights, while also promoting the internationalization of IP through Patent Cooperation Treaty (PCT) international examinations. Its responsibilities extend to combating unfair competition and counterfeit goods. Key legislation under KIPO's purview includes the Patent Act, Utility Model Act, Design Protection Act, and Trademark Act.

Under KIPO is the **Intellectual Property Trial and Appeal Board (IPTAB, 특허심판원)**. The IPTAB handles disputes concerning the creation, modification, and invalidation of IP rights, such as patents and trademarks, through quasi-judicial processes. Although patent infringement lawsuits (seeking damages or injunctions) are managed by the general court system, the IPTAB handles matters concerning the scope or validity of rights. Appeals from IPTAB decisions are directed to the Patent Court and, if necessary, the Supreme Court.

For legal counsels, **KIPRIS (Korea Intellectual Property Rights Information Service, 특허정보검색서비스)**, managed by KIPO, is an invaluable resource for searching and reviewing registered IP rights. KIPRIS is a free, user-friendly, and comprehensive search service for industrial property rights such as patents, trademarks, utility models, and designs in Korea.

- **National Tax Service (NTS, 국세청)**

The National Tax Service (NTS) is Korea's primary tax authority, similar to the Internal Revenue Service (IRS) in the U.S. While operating under the Ministry of Economy and Finance (MOEF), the NTS functions with a degree of independence, much like the KIPO under its respective ministry. The NTS oversees the collection and administration of national taxes, including income tax, corporate tax, value-added tax, and inheritance tax. In contrast, customs duties are managed by the Korea Customs Service, another independent organization under the MOEF, while local taxes are handled by local governments.

The NTS has two primary roles: supporting taxpayers and enforcing tax compliance. It assists taxpayers by providing guidance, interpreting tax laws, and offering help with tax filings. On the enforcement side, the NTS identifies non-compliance and ensures tax collection through investigations and enforcement actions.

For most companies, routine tax matters, such as corporate tax filings, are typically managed by the finance department. However, legal teams may interact with the NTS in specific cases. For example, companies in regulated industries, such as the liquor industry, need licenses from tax authorities, and the NTS offers dedicated support for this. The NTS also operates Hometax(홈택스), an online platform that businesses use for registrations, tax filings and obtaining certificates, which may occasionally involve legal teams.

If a taxpayer disputes a tax decision, they can appeal through the Tax Tribunal (조세심판원), an independent body under the Prime Minister's office that handles both national and local tax disputes. Unlike in the U.S., where a separate tax court exists, Korea has no dedicated tax court. After appealing through the Tax Tribunal, dissatisfied taxpayers must take their case to the Administrative Court, not a tax court.

THE EVOLVING STRUCTURE

Corporate legal counsel often engages with government organizations far more than litigators, whose primary interactions are with courts and prosecutors. This section has provided an overview of several key government bodies—such as the KFTC, FSC, MOEL, KIPO, and NTS—that are essential in corporate legal practice.

It's crucial to recognize that these organizations are not static. They evolve in response to societal needs and changing priorities. For example, the Korea Disease Control and Prevention Agency (KDCA) was elevated from the Korea Centers for Disease Control, a smaller bureau under the Ministry of Health and Welfare. This transformation, prompted by the COVID-19 pandemic, reflects the heightened importance of public health, with the KDCA now operating as an independent agency on par with KIPO and NTS.

Such restructuring illustrates how the government adapts to shifting societal priorities. The ongoing debate surrounding the Ministry of Gender Equality and Family provides another example. Some argue for its dissolution and absorption into a larger ministry, while others advocate for its continued independence, emphasizing its significance in addressing gender equality and family issues. The structure of government organizations reflects the values of the time. As these values shift, so do the organizations tasked with implementing them. Understanding this fluidity is essential for legal professionals. Government structures mirror the values of their time, and staying attuned to these shifts enables legal practitioners to navigate Korea's legal, administrative, and cultural landscape effectively.

Bullet Point Summary

- **Overview of the Executive Branch**: The executive branch, led by the President and supported by the Prime Minister, is responsible for executing laws and managing state affairs. Ministries, commissions, and independent agencies carry out specialized functions. Key ministries include the Ministry of Justice (MOJ), Ministry of Economy and Finance (MOEF), and Ministry of Employment and Labor (MOEL). For in-house counsels, understanding the executive branch is critical since corporate legal work often revolves around regulatory compliance, licensing, and interactions with administrative bodies. Unlike litigators who primarily engage with judges and prosecutors, in-house lawyers frequently deal with agencies like the KFTC, FSC, and MOEL, whose actions directly impact business operations and risk management.

- **Key Regulatory Bodies Shaping Corporate Practice**:

  Korea Fair Trade Commission (KFTC): Regulates antitrust matters, merger reviews, consumer protection, and fair trade practices, much like the U.S. FTC.

  Financial Services Commission (FSC) and Financial Supervisory Service (FSS): The FSC creates financial policy, while the FSS ensures compliance, managing banking, securities, and capital markets.

  Ministry of Employment and Labor (MOEL): Oversees labor policies, workplace safety, and employment laws, consolidating functions handled by multiple U.S. agencies.

  Korean Intellectual Property Office (KIPO): Administers patents, trademarks, and IP disputes, operating like USPTO.

  National Tax Service (NTS): Handles tax compliance and administration through tools like Hometax, similar to the IRS, while tax disputes are resolved through the Tax Tribunal.

- **Evolving Administrative Structure:** Government bodies adapt to societal needs, as demonstrated by the KDCA's rise from a bureau to an independent agency during the COVID-19 pandemic.

CHAPTER 3. CORPORATE LAW

SECTION 1. BASICS OF CORPORATE LAW

THERE IS NO single statute titled 'Corporate Law' in Korea. Instead, corporate law is structured primarily around the **Commercial Act (상법)**, which serves as the fundamental legal framework governing business entities. This statute forms the backbone of corporate activities, outlining the types of companies, share structures, and key corporate documents. It also lays out regulations aimed at ensuring transparency, protecting shareholder rights, and maintaining legal compliance. For listed companies, additional laws, such as the **Financial Investment Services and Capital Markets Act (자본시장과 금융투자업에 관한 법률, 자본시장법)**, introduce further requirements related to disclosure, financial standards, and governance, addressing the unique nature of publicly traded companies.

THE CORE: THE COMMERCIAL ACT (상법)

The **Commercial Act**, enacted in 1963, is the cornerstone of corporate law in Korea. Chapter 3, titled Company, forms the core framework for corporations, similar to how the Delaware General Corporation Law (DGCL) governs corporations in the U.S. It establishes essential principles governing business entities, share structures, corporate governance, and operations.

The Commercial Act is divided into six chapters: **General Provisions, Commercial Transactions, Company, Insurance, Maritime Commerce,** and **Air Carriage**, covering a broad range of business activities. In terms of legal hierarchy, special laws take precedence over the Commercial Act, followed by commercial customs and Civil Act, ensuring consistent application of specialized regulations.

Korea's corporate law draws influence from U.S. corporate law, particularly the DGCL, in areas such as corporate formation, capital raising, and mergers. However, while the DGCL relies heavily on case law for interpretation, the Korean Commercial Act takes a more prescriptive approach, with specific statutory provisions guiding corporate governance and activities. Both systems, though different, aim to balance corporate flexibility with stakeholder protection.

ADDITIONAL REGULATORY LAYERS

Beyond the Commercial Act, other key statutes regulate corporate activities, particularly for listed companies, financial audits, and fair trade. The **Financial Investment Services and Capital Markets Act (자본시장과 금융투자업에 관한 법률, 자본시장법)** sets forth the disclosure requirements and financial standards that publicly traded companies must follow to protect investors and maintain market integrity. The **Act on External Audit of Stock Companies (주식회사 등의 외부감사에 관한 법률, 외감법)** mandates external audits for certain businesses, enhancing transparency and accountability. It delegates the responsibility of setting accounting standards to the Financial Services Commission and, by extension, the **Korea Accounting Standards Board (KASB)**, influencing accounting practices across the industries. The **Monopoly Regulation and Fair Trade Act (독점규제 및 공정거래에 관한 법률, 공정거래법)** addresses the structure and operations of holding companies, placing restrictions on mutual investments to ensure a competitive and fair market environment. Meanwhile, the **Debtor Rehabilitation and Bankruptcy Act (채무자 회생 및 파산에 관한 법률,**

파산법) complements the **Commercial Act** by providing mechanisms for corporate restructuring and bankruptcy, ensuring an orderly approach to insolvency. Additional regulations, such as the **Bank Act** and **Insurance Business Act**, apply to specific industries and add further layers of regulation.

Korea's corporate law framework can be seen as a complex jigsaw puzzle, with each statute—from the **Commercial Act** to **the Financial Investment Services and Capital Markets Act**—serving as an essential piece that shapes the overall legal landscape for businesses. Together, they form an integrated system that governs corporate conduct in Korea.

In the sections to follow, we will explore the different types of companies, such as Chusik Hoesa and walk through the key steps involved in establishing a corporation. We will also examine essential corporate documents like the Corporate Registry, Articles of Incorporation, and Business Registration. By the end of this section, you will have a practical understanding of company formation, operation, and regulation in Korea, providing a solid foundation for corporate legal practice.

Bullet Point Summary

- **No Stand-Alone Corporate Law**: Korea has no single statute titled "Corporate Law." Instead, corporate governance is primarily regulated under the Commercial Act (상법) with a chapter titled Company, outlining company structures, share frameworks, and governance principles.

- **Additional Regulations for Corporate Activities:** Other statutes, such as the Financial Investment Services and Capital Markets Act and the Fair Trade Act, complement the Commercial Act, ensuring comprehensive oversight, particularly for listed companies and fair competition. Together, they form an integrated system shaping business operations.

SECTION 2. TYPES OF COMPANIES AND SHARES

NATURAL PERSON VS JURISTIC PERSON

BEFORE DIVING INTO the various types of companies, it's important to distinguish between a "natural person" and a "juristic person", as defined in the Civil Act. A natural person refers to an individual human being—with real flesh, blood, and inherent legal rights and responsibilities. On the other hand, a juristic person is a legal entity, such as a corporation or organization, recognized by law as having its own legal identity. This means juristic persons can own property, pay taxes, enter into contracts, and conduct business independently of the people involved. They can also be sued or even face criminal charges, reflecting their distinct status under the law.

The Civil Act primarily deals with non-profit juristic persons, focusing on entities established for purposes other than making a profit. In contrast, the Commercial Act governs the formation and management of companies (회사), which are profit-making juristic persons. This is similar to the legal framework in other jurisdictions, where corporations are treated as separate from their owners. This separation provides what is known as "limited liability," protecting shareholders from being personally liable for corporate debts—a crucial concept in corporate governance and liability. With this distinction in mind, let's move on to the types of companies recognized under Korean law, each with unique characteristics and legal requirements.

TYPES OF COMPANIES: CHUSIK-HOESA AND BEYOND

Businesses can choose from various corporate structures, each catering to specific operational and strategic needs. These include the Joint Stock Company (주식회사, Chusik Hoesa), Limited Liability Company (유한회사, Yuhan Hoesa), Limited Liability Partnership (유한책임회사, Yuhan Chaegim Hoesa), General Partnership Company (합명회사, Hapmyeong Hoesa), and Limited Partnership Company (합자회사, Hapja Hoesa). Among these, Chusik Hoesa, comparable to a C corporation in the U.S., and Yuhan Hoesa, akin to an LLC, dominate Korea's business landscape and are the focus of the following discussions.

Number of Companies by Type (as of 2022, according to the National Tax Service Statistics)

Joint Stock Company	893,485 (95%)
Limited Liability Company	42,869 (4.6%)
Limited Partnership Company	2,987 (0.3%)
General Partnership Company	950 (0.1%)
Total	942,144

▪ Joint Stock Company (주식회사, Chusik-hoesa)

Chusik Hoesa is the preferred structure for businesses seeking growth through external investments. It offers shareholders limited liability while allowing the issuance of various types of shares and bonds. A key feature is the distinction between ownership (shareholders) and management (board of directors). The transferability of shares further enhances flexibility in ownership and investment.

Ownership in a Chusik Hoesa is represented by shares (주식), and the shareholders (주주) participate in Shareholders' Meetings (주주총회) to elect directors and approve major corporate decisions. Governance is managed by a Board of Directors (이사회), which oversees operations and strategic direction. Notably, Chusik Hoesa is the only corporate form eligible for public listing and trading on the stock exchange, making it the go-to option for companies planning to go public.

▪ **Limited Liability Company (유한회사, Yuhan-hoesa)**

Unlike Chusik Hoesa (Joint Stock Company), Yuhan Hoesa's ownership is divided into units (좌), with members (사원) participating in Members' Meetings (사원총회) for governance. Its simpler management structure and fewer formalities make it a preferred choice for small to medium-sized enterprises.

Historically, Yuhan Hoesa's private nature, exempt from public disclosure (공시) and external audits (외부감사), made it particularly attractive for foreign companies. Global firms like Google, Apple, and Microsoft opted to establish their Korean subsidiaries as Yuhan Hoesa to take advantage of these features. However, the 2018 reform to the Act on External Audit of Stock Companies (주식회사의 외부감사에 관한 법률) introduced mandatory disclosure and audit requirements for Yuhan Hoesa exceeding certain thresholds. Reflecting its expanded scope, the act was renamed the Act on External Audit of Stock Companies, etc. (주식회사 등의 외부감사에 관한 법률) to explicitly include Yuhan Hoesa under its provisions. Since the reform took effect, entities like Google Korea now comply with these requirements, aligning them more closely with publicly accountable companies.

While the reform tightened oversight of Yuhan Hoesa, it did not extend to Yuhan Chaegim Hoesa (Limited Liability Partnership, 유한책임회사). This gap led some foreign subsidiaries to exploit the exemption by restructuring their corporate form through the organizational change process (조직변경) under the Commercial Act (Article 604). Recognizing this loophole, as of 2024, the National Assembly is deliberating amendments to the External Audit Act to bring Yuhan Chaegim Hoesa under its purview as well, further aligning regulatory practices.

Choosing between Chusik Hoesa and Yuhan Hoesa is not merely a matter of legal formality but a strategic decision influenced by factors such as the company's size, investment goals, and the desired balance between operational simplicity and regulatory obligations.

- **Branch Office ['지점' according to the Foreign Exchange Transaction Act , '영업소' according to the Commercial Act]**

Strictly speaking, a branch office (지점) is not a type of company. However, it is included in the "Types of Companies" section because it is a common option for foreign companies aiming to conduct business in Korea.

Foreign companies typically choose between establishing a foreign investment company (외국인투자기업) or setting up a branch office (외국기업 국내지점), depending on their strategic needs. A foreign investment company operates as an independent legal entity, akin to a hiker's child who treks alongside the parent but with their own identity. Registered under the Foreign Investment Promotion Act (외국인투자촉진법), such companies enjoy benefits like tax incentives and easier fund remittance upon meeting a minimum investment threshold (KRW 100 million as of 2024). The parent company is not directly liable for its debts, granting legal and financial separation.

In contrast, a branch office functions as an operational extension of its foreign parent company, similar to a hiker's backpack. Essential yet not independent, the backpack moves wherever the hiker goes. In the same way, a branch office, registered as a business office

(영업소) under the Commercial Act, remains tied to the parent entity. Financial transactions, including fund transfers and profit repatriation, are governed by the Foreign Exchange Transaction Act (외국환거래법) and require reporting to designated foreign exchange banks.

Choosing between a foreign investment company and a branch office is like deciding between citizenship and a green card. Both offer similar benefits and obligations, but with key differences. Each option has its own set of benefits and legal implications, making it essential to understand their differences based on the specific needs and strategic goals of the business.

TYPES OF SHARES: COMMON, PREFERRED, AND MORE

The principle of the homogeneity of shares, as stipulated in Korean corporate law, asserts that all shares should possess equal rights. This principle ensures fairness and uniformity in shareholder treatment. However, to meet diverse business needs and investor preferences, Article 344 of the Commercial Act permits the issuance of different classes of shares, deviating from this principle to offer flexibility in corporate financing and governance. The issuance of such shares must be explicitly authorized in the company's Articles of Incorporation.

- **Common Shares (보통주)**

Common shares represent the basic equity stake in a company, granting holders voting rights and a claim to the company's profits through dividends. While they confer voting rights, financial claims—such as dividends and liquidation proceeds—are subordinate to those of preferred shareholders and creditors, making common shares the foundation of corporate equity but secondary in financial priority.

- **Class Shares (종류주식) and Preferred Shares (우선주)**

Class shares, including preferred shares, serve specific corporate strategies and investor preferences. Preferred shares typically take precedence over common shares in dividend payouts and asset claims during liquidation. They often include features like conversion rights (전환권), enabling holders to convert their shares into another class, and redemption rights (상환권), allowing or obligating the company to repurchase shares at predetermined terms. These features provide flexibility in financial and strategic planning, catering to diverse investor needs and corporate growth phases.

When multiple types of preferred shares are issued, they are categorized as 'Type 1 Preferred Shares' (1종 우선주), 'Type 2 Preferred Shares' (2종 우선주), and so on, with details disclosed in the Corporate Registry (법인등기부) for transparency and governance purposes.

Korean corporate law used to prohibit shares with veto rights (거부권부주식), director appointment or dismissal rights (임원임면권부주식), or multiple voting rights (복수의결권주식). However, recent amendments to the Act on Special Measures for the Promotion of Venture Businesses (벤처기업육성에 관한 특별조치법) now permit venture companies to issue shares with multiple voting rights. This change allows founders to retain control while raising capital, reflecting the evolving landscape of corporate governance in Korea.

- **Investment Instruments: SAFE (조건부지분인수계약) and Convertible Notes (조건부지분전환계약)**

SAFE, a popular investment instrument initially developed in Silicon Valley, allows startups to raise capital without immediate dilution of ownership and provides investors with the right to acquire equity in the future under predefined conditions. Convertible Notes, combining features of debt and equity financing, convert into equity under specified conditions, facilitating smoother funding rounds by delaying valuation negotiations until later funding rounds. These instruments were formally introduced through amendments to the Venture Investment Promotion Act (벤처투자 촉진에 관한 법률). Their adoption underscores Korea's commitment to fostering a dynamic investment environment while maintaining stringent governance standards to protect shareholders and uphold corporate integrity.

Bullet Point Summary

- **Natural Person vs. Juristic Person:** A natural person refers to an individual human being, while a juristic person is a legally recognized entity, such as a corporation, capable of owning property, entering contracts, and bearing liabilities.

- **Types of Companies:** Korean law recognizes five types of companies, but this section focuses on Chusik Hoesa and Yuhan Hoesa, as they are the most commonly used in Korea's business environment.

  Chusik Hoesa: Preferred for larger corporations, it offers transferable shares, eligibility for public listing, and governance through a Board of Directors.

  Yuhan Hoesa: Suited for SMEs, it features private ownership with a simpler governance structure, though recent reforms introduced disclosure and audit requirements for larger entities.

  Branch Offices: While not strictly a type of company, branch offices allow foreign companies to operate in Korea without establishing a separate legal entity, making them a common alternative to foreign investment companies.

- **Types of Shares:**

  Common Shares: Represent basic equity stakes with voting rights but secondary claims in dividends and liquidation.

  Class Shares: Include preferred shares with features such as conversion rights and redemption rights, offering flexibility in corporate financing. Preferred shares can be categorized as 'Type 1 Preferred Shares', 'Type 2 Preferred Shares,' etc., with classifications disclosed in the corporate registry for transparency.

  Investment Instruments: While not strictly types of shares, SAFE and Convertible Notes provide innovative funding options for startups, balancing investor preferences with corporate governance standards.

SECTION 3. INCORPORATION AND CORPORATE DOCUMENTS

ESTABLISHING A COMPANY: A PROCEDURAL WALKTHROUGH

BUILDING ON OUR discussion of company types and share classes, this section outlines the procedural steps for establishing a company in Korea, using a **Joint Stock Company (주식회사, Chusik Hoesa)** as the example.

Step 1: Corporate Registration

1. Choose a Business Name: Select a business name in Korean that is not already registered for a similar type of business in the same district. For instance, although Facebook rebranded to Meta globally, its Korean subsidiary remains as Facebook Korea because "Meta Co., Ltd." was already registered in Seoul for a similar business.

2. Determine Capital Amount(자본금) and Share Par Value (액면가): Decide the par value of each share and the total num-

ber of shares to issue, as these determine the company's registered capital amount. For example, issuing 10,000 shares at a par value of 500 KRW results in a registered capital amount of 5 million KRW. If 1,000 additional shares are later issued at 10,000 KRW per share, raising 10 million KRW, the registered capital amount increases only by the par value of the new shares. The corporate registry will reflect a capital amount of 5.5 million KRW (initial 5 million KRW + 1,000 shares x 500 KRW par value). The difference between the par value and the issuance price—9.5 million KRW—is recorded as capital surplus (자본잉여금) in the financial statements but is not reflected in the corporate registry.

3. Define Business Purpose(사업목적), Business Address (주소지), shareholders (주주) and executives (임원): Gather this essential information to draft the Articles of Incorporation and other necessary documents for filing with the registration office.

4. File documents with the Commercial Registration Office (등기소): Collect and submit various corporate documents to the commercial registration office. The following list outlines the documents needed. Once filed, the corporate registry is typically completed within a few business days, legally establishing the company. A juristic person (법인) is thus 'born.'

- Application for Incorporation Registration (설립등기 신청서)
- Founders' Meeting Minutes (발기인회 의사록)
- Consent Form for Shortening the Founders' Meeting Period (발기인회 기간단축 동의서)
- Consent Form for Share Issuance (주식발행사항동의서)
- Articles of Incorporation (정관)
- Stock Subscription Certificate (주식인수증)
- Acceptance of Appointment (취임승낙서)
- Investigation Report (조사보고서)

- Balance Certificate (잔액증명서)
- Corporate Seal Registration Certificate (법인인감신고서)

Step 2: Tax Registration and Others

1. Register with the Tax Office: After completing corporate registration, the company must register with the tax office to obtain a business registration certificate. This step is a legal prerequisite for commencing business operations. Required documents include the Articles of Incorporation, Shareholder Registry, and Corporate Registration Certificate, among others.

2. Obtain Licenses and Permits: Additional licenses or permits may be necessary depending on the industry. For instance, a waste management business requires approval from the Ministry of Environment under Article 25 of the Waste Control Act. The National Tax Service's HomeTax platform can help identify whether a specific business type requires licensing. By entering the business code, users can determine whether additional permits are needed and find related guidance on required documentation, governing laws, and filing locations.

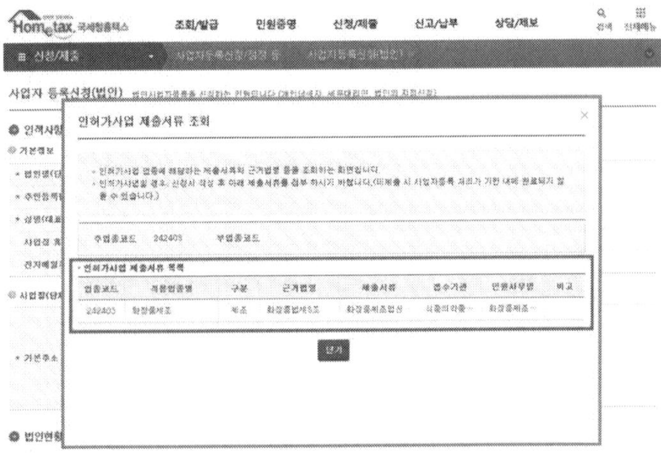

3. Open Corporate Bank Account: Select a bank of your choice. Most banks will require the business registration certificate and identification documents for account setup.

4. Register for Social Insurance: It is mandatory for employers in Korea to register for social insurance, which includes national health insurance, national pension, and employment insurance. Tax advisors typically manage these registrations to ensure compliance with regulatory requirements.

Establishing a company involves numerous administrative tasks that can be complex and time-consuming. Services like helpXX and jobXX—comparable to LegalZoom in the U.S.—offer comprehensive support for tasks such as drafting incorporation documents and filing with the corporate registry. By leveraging such services, businesses can ensure accuracy and efficiency while focusing on strategic objectives.

BASIC CORPORATE DOCUMENTS: CORNERSTONES OF LEGALITY

Managing and reviewing basic corporate documents might seem straightforward—indeed, in large law firms, these tasks are often delegated to administrative staff rather than attorneys. However, for in-house and corporate lawyers, understanding these documents is critically important. Much of your daily work will revolve around maintaining, interpretating or explaining these documents, rather than engaging with complex legal theories or court rulings. Just as individuals carry essential forms of identification such as resident registration cards or driver's licenses, companies rely on corporate documents to affirm their legal identity and operational authority. These documents form the backbone of corporate governance and operational compliance, encapsulating the legal framework within which a company operates. Interestingly, this practical knowledge is often overlooked in traditional legal education; for example, I first encountered the 'corporate registry' not in law school, but during a legal due diligence assignment at my first law firm. Below is a summary of key corporate documents, their functions, and guidance on how to access them.

1. Corporate Registry (법인등기부): The corporate registry serves as the official record of a company's existence, akin to a Certificate of Incorporation in the U.S. Maintained by the commercial registration office, it contains critical information such as the company's name, address, share structure, capital amount, and details about directors and executives. Any changes to the corporate structure—such as capital increases or shifts in management—must be promptly updated in the registry. Failure to do so can result in administrative penalties. Official copies of the registry can be obtained via the online commercial registration system (IROS).

2. Articles of Incorporation (정관): Often described as the "constitution" of the company, the Articles of Incorporation outline the company's purpose, governance structure, and operational guidelines. They serve as a hybrid of the Articles of Incorporation and Bylaws in the U.S. and are filed during the initial registration process.

3. Business Registration Certificate (사업자등록증): Issued by the National Tax Service (NTS) following tax registration, this certificate is comparable to a Business License in the U.S. It serves as proof of tax registration and is essential for legal business operations. Copies can be obtained through the NTS's online platform.

4. Corporate Seal (법인인감) and Corporate Seal Certificate (법인인감증명서): The corporate seal is a registered stamp

used to validate official documents. A Corporate Seal Certificate confirms its authenticity and is frequently required for contracts, especially those involving government entities or major transactions.

5. Shareholder Registry (주주명부): Similar to the Stock Ledger in the U.S., this document lists all the company's shareholders and is essential for maintaining transparency in ownership and voting rights. The company regularly updates it to reflect any changes in share ownership.

6. Minutes of Shareholders' Meetings (주주총회의사록) and Board Meetings (이사회의사록): These records document the proceedings and decisions made during shareholder and board meetings. They are critical for legal compliance, particularly for validating decisions on major agendas such as capital increases or changes in directorship.

7. Rules of Employment (취업규칙): Required for companies with 10 or more employees, this document outlines employment terms such as working hours, holidays, and policies. Comparable to an Employee Handbook in the U.S., it serves as the cornerstone of HR policies. The Ministry of Employment and Labor provides a recommended template for compliance.

8. Other Permits, Licenses, and Certificates: Depending on the business sector and activities, additional permits and certificates may be required. Examples include the Foreign Investment Enterprise Certificate (외국인투자기업등록증명서), Venture Business Certificate (벤처기업확인서), and Online Sales Report Certificate (통신판매신고증). These documents validate the company's compliance with specific regulatory requirements and enable certain business activities.

Bullet Point Summary

- **Establishing a Company:** Incorporating a company in Korea begins with corporate registration, followed by tax registration and obtaining necessary permits or licenses.

  Corporate registration involves submitting required documents, such as Articles of Incorporation, to the commercial registration office. The corporate registry, available at www.iros.go.kr, records details like the company's name, capital amount, and directors.

  Tax registration with the National Tax Service (NTS) through the Hometax website is essential for obtaining a business registration certificate and legally commencing operations.

  For certain industries, additional licenses may be required, which can be checked using the Hometax website's industry code tool.

- **Basic Corporate Documents**: Companies maintain essential records to ensure legal compliance and smooth governance, including:

  The **corporate registry**, updated to reflect changes in the company's structure.

  The **business registration certificate**, proof of tax registration.

  The **corporate seal** and accompanying seal certificate, required especially for public sector contracts.

  The **rules of employment** for companies with more than 10 employees, with templates available on the Ministry of Employment and Labor's website.

SECTION 4. DIRECTOR LIABILITY, SHAREHOLDER RIGHTS AND CORPORATE GOVERNANCE

THE DUTIES AND liabilities of directors, along with shareholders' rights, are primarily outlined in the Commercial Act. Unlike the incorporation procedure and corporate documents discussed earlier, these topics are typically covered in law school under Corporate Law, although for in-house counsels, these issues may not arise frequently unless they work in listed Korean companies or within a compliance team. Nonetheless, a solid understanding of these fundamentals is crucial. They provide a foundation for grasping daily legal news and discussions involving compliance and corporate governance, which should be understood within the broader context of Korean society, history, and economic structure.

DUTIES AND LIABILITIES OF DIRECTORS

Directors of Korean corporations owe fiduciary duties to the corporation, as outlined in the Commercial Act. These duties fall primarily into two categories: the duty of care and the duty of loyalty.

Duty of Care

The duty of care requires directors to exercise the same level of diligence that an ordinarily prudent person is expected to provide in performing their duties (Article 382 of the Commercial Act). Korean courts recognize the Business Judgment Rule as a defense against allegations of breach, even in cases involving conflicts of interest, as long as the actions do not involve illegal conduct. This is a notable departure from U.S. standards, where the Business Judgment Rule is generally unavailable in conflict-of-interest situations. As a result, directors in Korea may find it easier to defend their decisions, even in challenging circumstances, provided they act within the bounds of legality.

Duty of Loyalty

The duty of loyalty ensures directors act in the best interest of the corporation. This duty is codified in the Commercial Act, which prohibits directors from competing with the corporation, appropriating corporate opportunities for personal gain, or engaging in self-dealing transactions (Articles 397, 397-2, and 398 of the Commercial Act). However, these acts are not completely prohibited but require prior board approval.

In Korea, most large corporations are part of chaebols—business groups like Samsung, Hyundai, and SK—that involve complex networks of affiliated companies. This structure makes related-party transactions and self-dealing prevalent. Article 398 of the Commercial Act, which governs self-dealing, is frequently invoked to address these conflicts. However, the effectiveness of this provision is often undermined by boards controlled by individuals closely aligned with the controlling families, limiting their ability to ensure fair transactions. This reflects broader challenges in Korean corporate governance, where achieving transparency and fairness remains an ongoing effort.

Civil and Criminal Liabilities

Directors can face civil liabilities to the corporation, liabilities to third parties, and criminal liabilities for breaches of their duties:

- Liabilities to the Corporation

Directors are liable to the corporation for damages resulting from breaches of law or duties that cause financial harm (Article 399 of the Commercial Act). Examples include selling corporate assets below market value, embezzling funds, or granting unsecured loans. These breaches can lead to lawsuits brought either by the corporation directly or by shareholders through derivative actions.

- Liabilities to Third Parties

Directors are also liable to third parties who suffer losses due to intentional or grossly negligent actions (Article 401 of the Commercial Act). For example, a director who manipulates financial statements could be held accountable if a creditor provides a loan based on those false statements. However, the burden of proving gross negligence lies with the third party. Liability extends to shadow directors (Article 401-2), including individuals who influence the corporation without holding formal titles, such as family members of chaebol owners.

- Criminal Liabilities

A notable tendency in Korea is the frequent use of criminal charges against directors. Under the Criminal Act, directors can face criminal fines and sentences for breaches of trust (Article 355 of the Criminal Act). Due to the lack of punitive damages and discovery systems, civil actions are less effective in preventing misconduct. Prosecutors often address this gap by applying criminal breach of trust charges to various misconducts by directors, officers, and controlling shareholders. Additionally, recent laws like the Serious Accident Punishment Act impose criminal liabilities on representative directors for safety violations and accidents.

SHAREHOLDER RIGHTS AND CORPORATE GOVERNANCE

Shareholders in Korea are granted a comprehensive set of rights under the Commercial Act, categorized primarily into voting rights, rights to participate in major corporate decisions, preemptive rights, and the right to pursue directors' liabilities through derivative actions. While robust on paper, the practical exercise of these rights often faces significant challenges.

Voting and Participation in Corporate Decisions

Shareholders wield their voting power during shareholder meetings to influence critical corporate decisions. Key matters requiring shareholder resolutions include the election and removal of directors (Articles 382 and 385 of the Commercial Act), approval of stock option grants (Article 340-2), decisions on capital reduction, mergers, acquisitions, comprehensive stock swaps, and other significant structural changes. For dissenting shareholders in mergers or stock swaps, the law provides appraisal rights (put options), enabling them to sell their shares back to the company if they disagree with the resolution. Additionally, shareholders approve the aggregate ceiling for directors' remuneration (Article 388). While this appears to give shareholders significant control, in practice, many corporations approve an annual firm-wide ceiling for the aggregate amount of director remuneration, limiting the actual power of shareholders over individual director salaries.

Since voting rights are exercised only during convened shareholder meetings and pertain solely to agenda items presented, the ability to convene extraordinary shareholder meetings and propose agenda items is critical. Shareholders with at least 3% of total issued shares

(1% for listed companies) can request the board to convene an extraordinary meeting. This ensures minority shareholders can raise concerns and propose significant issues for deliberation.

Derivative Actions and Preemptive Rights

Shareholders holding 1% of total issued shares (0.01% if listed) may bring derivative actions against directors on behalf of the corporation (Article 403(1) of the Commercial Act). Due to the lack of a U.S.-style discovery process, derivative actions frequently follow criminal prosecutions or administrative inspections, to leverage findings from these proceedings to support the shareholder's case.

Shareholders also possess preemptive rights to purchase new shares on a pro-rata basis, to prevent dilution of their ownership. However, exceptions exist when there is a 'proper business purpose' (Article 418(2) of the Commercial Act), and in practice, challenging third-party share allocations is rare due to this broad exception.

Challenges to Exercising Shareholder Rights

On paper, shareholders in Korea have strong rights, including the ability to remove directors without cause, secured pro-rata rights, and derivative actions. However, significant hurdles exist in practice. High shareholding thresholds for exercising certain rights, the absence of a U.S.-style discovery system, and class actions (except for certain securities litigation case) and punitive damages limit the effectiveness of these rights. Consequently, shareholders rely more on criminal charges than civil actions, which may explain the strong power of the prosecutors' office extending to corporate governance issues.

Note: Chaebol (Large Business Groups)

Large business groups, or chaebols, dominate Korea's corporate landscape. These family-controlled conglomerates—such as Samsung, Hyundai, LG, and SK—comprise interconnected companies spanning diverse industries. Despite often holding relatively small equity stakes, 'owner families' maintain disproportionate control through mechanisms like holding companies and circular shareholding structures. This concentration of power often leads to governance issues, including tunneling—where wealth is shifted within the group to benefit the controlling family at the expense of minority shareholders. Due to limitations in Korea's corporate, civil law—such as the absence of punitive damages and class actions—criminal penalties and competition law are the primary tools used to regulate these practices.

Bullet Point Summary

Duties and Liabilities of Directors:

- Directors in Korea have fiduciary duties of care and loyalty under the Commercial Act, requiring them to act prudently and prioritize the corporation's best interests. The business judgment rule provides a defense for decisions made in good faith, though its application differs from the U.S.

- Related party transactions, common within chaebols, are governed by provisions like Article 398 of the Commercial Act. However, board approvals often fail to ensure true fairness due to close ties with controlling families.

- Directors may face civil liability to the corporation or third parties for negligence or breaches, as well as criminal liability for misconduct.

Shareholder Rights and Corporate Governance:

- Shareholders enjoy voting rights, appraisal rights in mergers, preemptive rights to prevent dilution, and the ability to bring derivative actions against directors. These rights, while robust on paper, face practical limitations due to high thresholds and the absence of class actions or punitive damages. Derivative actions often rely on findings from criminal or administrative investigations due to the absence of a discovery process.

- Chaebols, family-controlled conglomerates, dominate Korea's corporate landscape, often leading to governance challenges like tunneling. Regulatory responses rely heavily on criminal penalties and competition law due to limitations in civil remedies.

CHAPTER 4.
CONTRACTS

SECTION 1. BASICS OF CONTRACT LAW

THE KOREAN CONTRACT CANVAS

KOREA DOES NOT have a standalone statute titled "Contract Law." Instead, contractual principles are governed by the Civil Act, which provides the foundational legal framework, and the Commercial Act, which addresses the specific needs of business and commercial agreements. Together, these statutes allow businesses significant flexibility to define their terms, including the scope of services, pricing, and payment methods, while ensuring fairness and adherence to legal boundaries.

A unique feature of Korean contract law is the absence of a requirement for consideration or specific formalities. Gratuitous contracts without consideration are enforceable, and agreements can be made orally or in writing. Additionally, the parol evidence rule—common in some jurisdictions to restrict extrinsic evidence in interpreting written contracts—is not recognized in Korea. Despite these differences, the fundamental principle remains the same: mutual agreement, or the "meeting of minds," forms the cornerstone of enforceable contracts.

The Civil Act outlines key elements such as mutual consent, performance obligations, breach of contract, and remedies, providing a comprehensive framework for contractual obligations. Complementing this, the Commercial Act governs specialized business transactions, addressing topics like agency agreements, brokerage, and commercial guarantees to reflect the unique needs of the corporate landscape.

Beyond these general frameworks, specific statutes regulate certain types of contracts. Residential and commercial leases are governed by the Housing Lease Protection Act (주택임대차보호법) and the Commercial Building Lease Protection Act (상가임대차보호법), offering lessees critical protections. The Act on the Regulation of Terms and Conditions (약관의 규제에 관한 법률) promotes fairness in standard contract terms, curbing abuses of unequal bargaining power. Similarly, the Fair Transactions in Subcontracting Act (하도급거래공정화에 관한 법률) safeguards subcontractors from unfair practices, which are especially prevalent in industries like construction and manufacturing.

This section will explore both the theory and practical aspects of contract formation and enforcement. It offers insights on drafting, reviewing, and managing contracts, along with practical tips for effectively using popular contract templates in day-to-day corporate practice.

KEY PROVISIONS IN THE CIVIL ACT

The Civil Act classifies contracts into 14 distinct types, providing detailed provisions for each. However, these specific rules often take a backseat in practice, as more specialized laws typically govern particular contracts. For instance, employment contracts fall under the purview of the Labor Standards Act, while lease agreements, though addressed in the Civil Act, are primarily regulated by the

Housing Lease Protection Act or the Commercial Building Lease Protection Act.

Therefore, this section focuses not on the individual contract types detailed in the Civil Act but on provisions crucial to contract enforcement. Key topics include non-performance, remedies for breach, and the legal consequences of contract violations. These provisions may not be needed for day-to-day contract reviews but become essential when addressing disputes or understanding court interpretations in enforcement scenarios. Additionally, I will highlight a few practical clauses in the Civil Act that, while often overlooked in legal education, are frequently encountered in real-world contract negotiations.

Article 390 (Non-performance of Obligations and Compensation for Damages)

If an obligor fails to effect performance in accordance with the tenor and purport of the obligation, the obligee may claim damages: Provided, That this shall not apply to where performance has become impossible and where this is not due to the obligor's intention or negligence.

This article establishes the basic principle that if a party fails to fulfill their contractual obligations, the other party is entitled to claim damages. In practice, you will not often refer to this provision when reviewing contracts. Most contracts explicitly restate these principles. Still, it often serves as the foundation for court rulings in breach of contract cases. For litigators, citing this article reinforces that parties are liable for failing to meet their obligations, though contracts usually restate these principles.

Article 393 (Scope of Compensation for Damage)

1. The compensation for damage arising from the non-performance of an obligation shall be limited to ordinary damages.

2. The obligor is responsible for reparation for damage that have arisen through special circumstances, only if he had foreseen or could have foreseen such circumstances.

This provision limits damages to ordinary losses unless special circumstances were foreseen by the breaching party. In practice, contracts often contain clauses that exclude indirect or special damages, such as "Neither party will be liable for lost profits or consequential damages." This statutory backing means that even if a contract does not explicitly limit liability for these types of damages, courts will typically rule out special damages unless it is proven that the other party foresaw or could have foreseen the circumstances leading to the damages.

Article 398 (Liquidated Damages)

1. The parties may determine in advance the amount of damages payable in the event of the non-performance of an obligation.
2. Where the amount of damages determined in advance is unduly excessive, the court may reduce the amount to a more reasonable and appropriate sum.
3. The agreement of a penalty is presumed to be determined in advance of the amount of damages.

Liquidated damages allow parties to set a fixed amount payable upon breach, simplifying enforcement and reducing uncertainty. However, if the agreed liquidated damages are excessively high, courts have the authority to reduce the amount to a more reasonable level. This helps ensure fairness in enforcement and prevents punitive financial consequences.

It's important for legal counsel to distinguish between **liquidated damages (손해배상액 예정)**, which compensate for actual losses, and **penalties (위약벌)**, which impose additional financial burdens beyond compensation. Ensuring that a liquidated damages clause is not interpreted as a penalty is crucial in contract negotiations, as penalties may carry harsher financial implications. Under Korean law, penalties are presumed to be pre-determined damages unless proven otherwise. This means that unless explicitly differentiated, a penalty clause may be treated as liquidated damages, and could be subject to court reduction if deemed excessive.

Article 741 (Definition of Unjust Enrichment)

A person who without any legal ground derives a benefit from the property or services of another and thereby causes loss to the latter shall be bound to return such benefit.

Article 750 (Definition of Torts)

Any person who causes losses to or inflicts injuries on another person by an unlawful act, intentionally or negligently, shall be bound to make compensation for damages arising therefrom.

These provisions apply where no valid contract exists or can serve as supplementary grounds for a claim if a breach of contract is not established. Article 741 covers situations where one party is unjustly enriched at the expense of another, while Article 750 provides for compensation in cases of unlawful conduct, whether intentional or negligent. Though these provisions are not usually the focus during contract reviews, they often arise in court rulings where contract validity is in question or where contract terms do not fully cover the damages in dispute. Furthermore, the methods of damage calculation used in tort claims are also useful in contract disputes, offering a valuable framework for assessing compensation when contractual terms are unclear or insufficient.

Article 379 (Legal Rate of Interest)

The rate of interest of a claim bearing interest, unless otherwise provided by other Acts or agreed by the parties, shall be five percent per annum.

> **Article 54 (Statutory Interest Rate in Commercial Activities)**
>
> The statutory interest rate on obligations arising out of commercial activities shall be six percent per annum.

While Article 379, which sets the legal rate of interest at five percent per annum (or six percent for obligations arising from commercial activities under the Commercial Act), may be viewed as a trivial provision in law school curricula, it proves to be quite useful in practical legal work. This rate becomes important when calculating interests on overdue payments or compensation for overdue obligations in the absence of a specified rate in the contract. For corporate attorneys, if a contract specifies an excessively high-interest rate, citing this provision can be a basis to negotiate a more reasonable rate, aligning with statutory norms.

KEY PROVISIONS IN OTHER STATUTES

Beyond the Civil Act, several statutes significantly influence contract review and negotiation, offering targeted guidance for specific agreements. These laws address fairness, compliance, and protections in areas like standardized terms, subcontracting, employment and commercial transactions.

The **Act on the Regulation of Standardized Terms and Conditions (약관의 규제에 관한 법률)** requires that standardized terms used in mass agreements be fair, transparent, and prepared in Korean for accessibility. Significant terms must be explained to the other party, or they may not be enforceable. For consumer-focused contracts, compliance with the **Personal Information Protection Act (개인정보 보호법)** is also critical, ensuring proper handling of personal data.

For practical guidance, legal counsels can refer to the contract templates provided by the Korea Fair Trade Commission (KFTC).

These widely used templates serve as a useful benchmark. If your terms are less favorable than the templates, they can be leveraged during negotiations to secure better terms.

The **Fair Transactions in Subcontracting Act (하도급거래 공정화에 관한 법률)** protects subcontractors, who often have less bargaining power than larger companies, from unfair practices by imposing restrictions on payment delays, unreasonable price reductions, and other exploitative terms. Legal counsels representing subcontractors should use these protections to negotiate better terms, while those representing principal contractors must ensure compliance to avoid legal disputes. The Act strongly recommends using KFTC-provided subcontract templates and requires Non-Disclosure Agreements (NDAs) to safeguard subcontractors' technology. While not mandatory, the KFTC's NDA template provides a reliable starting point for ensuring fairness and compliance.

In addition to the key statutes mentioned above, other laws may apply in specific contractual situations.

The **Commercial Act** contains provisions that can significantly impact various commercial agreements. For instance, **Article 41** restricts individuals from operating a competing business within the same or adjacent area for ten years after transferring their business. This provision requires careful review and negotiation in business transfer agreements. Additionally, **Article 92-2** supports claims for compensation by distributors based on their contribution to overall sales after the termination of a distribution agreement. Legal counsels can leverage these provisions to negotiate more favorable terms for their clients in distribution agreements.

The **Labor Standards Act** governs employment relationships and labor conditions, addressing critical areas such as employment contracts, working hours, wages, and termination procedures. In practice, many small and medium-sized businesses rely on contract templates provided by the Ministry of Employment and Labor, which serve as useful benchmarks for negotiations. These templates are widely accepted standards for reviewing and drafting employment contracts.

These statutes demonstrate the complexity and scope of contract law. However, there's no need to feel overwhelmed. Think of contract law as preparing a complex dish. Just as there are countless recipes for making kimchi, there are many ways to craft a legally compliant contract. Each statute and provision is like an ingredient—essential for enhancing the overall result, but not always strictly necessary. The more "ingredients" and techniques you understand, the more versatile and effective you will be in creating contracts that meet the needs of all parties involved. By mastering these statutes and provisions, you can tailor contracts that are both compliant and favorable, ensuring client's satisfaction while adhering to the law.

Bullet Point Summary

- Korea does not have a standalone statute titled "Contract Law." Instead, contractual principles are governed by the Civil Act, which provides foundational guidelines, and the Commercial Act, which addresses the specific needs of business and commercial agreements.

- Contracts in Korea are based on mutual agreement, without requiring consideration or formalities in theory. Think of contract law as preparing a complex dish—statutes and provisions, like ingredients, enhance the final result but are not always strictly necessary.

- Key statutes for contract review include: the Act on the Regulation of Terms and Conditions, ensuring fairness in standardized contracts; the Fair Transactions in Subcontracting Act, protecting subcontractors; the Personal Information Protection Act, regulating privacy compliance in contracts involving personal data; and the Housing Lease Protection Act and Commercial Building Lease Protection Act, governing lease agreements.

- Statutory tools such as the Commercial Act's provisions on competition restrictions and distributor compensation, along with government-provided templates from organizations like the Korea Fair Trade Commission (KFTC), serve as practical benchmarks for crafting legally compliant and fair agreements.

SECTION 2. MAJOR CONTRACTS

WHEN REVIEWING CONTRACTS governed by Korean law, the challenge often lies not in understanding the legal principles but in becoming familiar with commonly used templates and terms. While core principles—such as mutual consent, clear terms, and enforcement mechanisms—remain universal, the structure and common clauses in Korean contracts can differ significantly from those in U.S. or other jurisdictions. For example, clauses standard in U.S. contracts may be located in different sections or framed differently in Korean agreements.

While universal principles provide a foundation, specific nuances of Korean law require attention. This section will guide you through key Korean contract templates, highlighting important considerations and common clauses to be mindful of. By understanding these templates, you will gain a clearer sense of what to expect and what areas require particular focus during contract reviews.

1. EMPLOYMENT CONTRACT

Employment contracts in Korea require a written format—one of the few exceptions in a system where formality isn't always necessary. The Labor Standards Act mandates that these contracts be in writing, ensuring that both parties are clear on key elements like job description, working hours, and wages. The Ministry's standard one-page template, widely used by small businesses, simplifies this process by covering all necessary details. Notably, if any contract terms are less favorable to the employee than those prescribed by the **Labor Standards Act**, those terms are rendered invalid, with the Act's provisions taking precedence. You can access the Ministry's template here: https://www.moel.go.kr/mainpop2.do

Non-compete clauses are another key aspect of employment contracts. These clauses are particularly common for high-level professionals such as executives and managers. Unlike the recent FTC rule in the U.S. that restricts non-compete clauses for most workers, these clauses are still enforceable in Korea, though courts carefully assess their scope, duration, and fairness, considering the employee's position, length of employment, and whether any compensation was provided for agreeing to the clause. Generally, non-compete terms ranging from six months to one year are deemed reasonable, while longer durations may be considered excessive and invalid.

Termination of employment in Korea operates under the **"just cause" principle**, requiring a valid and substantial reason for dismissal. This is in stark contrast to the U.S. **"at-will" employment** doctrine, which allows termination for almost any reason (excluding discriminatory ones). Just cause typically involves serious misconduct, material breaches of contract, or comparable violations. Minor infractions or dissatisfaction with performance rarely meet the standard. If termination is challenged, the dispute often begins at the **Labor Commission (노동위원회)**, which provides a streamlined, accessible resolution process. Employers who fail to demonstrate just cause may face reinstatement orders or substantial financial penalties.

The **Labor Commission system** is an efficient alternative to traditional civil or criminal procedures. Initially designed to handle collective disputes, the LC is authorized to manage individual employment disputes, including unfair dismissal cases. The process is fast, accessible, and reasonable compared to traditional civil or criminal procedures. Disputes begin at the regional LC, where employees can file a complaint within 90 days of the incident. If unsatisfied with the regional LC's decision, they can escalate the matter to the national LC and appeal to the administrative court. This two-tiered system offers a structured yet flexible approach, ensuring that employee grievances are addressed promptly and fairly.

Employment contracts and regulations in Korea have been shaped by the country's rapid development, its relatively small size, culture dominated by collectivism, and the influence of large conglomerates (chaebols). The need to protect workers in this dynamic environment has led to robust legal regulations. The government supports compliance by offering tools and resources, reflecting a balanced approach that seeks to foster both business growth and worker protection.

2. NDA

Non-disclosure agreements (NDAs) in Korea generally follow a structure similar to those used in other jurisdictions. These agreements define confidential information, restrict its use, and require the return or disposal of the information. Compensation for breaches is typically addressed. The main differences are found in the governing law and dispute resolution clauses, which are based on Korean law and handled by Korean courts. Standard NDA terms range from three to five years, though they may align with a broader main agreement if applicable.

Korean NDAs often include one of three types of compensation clauses for breaches:

1. General Damages: The breaching party is liable for any damages caused. This is straightforward and typically acceptable.

2. Liquidated Damages: Specifies a set amount of compensation in the event of a breach, simplifying claims by removing the need to prove actual damages. Depending on your position, you may want to remove or negotiate the amount.

3. Penalty Clauses: These impose a penalty in addition to damages, without the need to prove losses. These clauses are particularly harsh for the recipient and should be negotiated or removed when possible, especially if you are representing the recipient.

For practical resources, the **Trade Secret Protection Center**, operated by the Korean Intellectual Property Office, provides NDA templates and guidelines tailored to protecting confidential information. Additionally, the **Fair Transactions in Subcontracting Act** mandates the execution of NDAs when subcontractors share proprietary technology. To comply with this requirement, the **Korea Fair Trade Commission (KFTC)** offers a standardized NDA template, which serves as a useful benchmark for drafting or reviewing agreements.

표준비밀유지계약서

(2022. . . 제정)

(Source: Cover of the NDA template offered by the KFTC)

3. SHARE TRANSFER AGREEMENT

A share transfer agreement typically includes key elements such as the number of shares being transferred, the price, payment terms, conditions precedent, representations and warranties, and closing procedures. These components form the core of the agreement. Parties can also negotiate additional terms to protect the purchaser's interests, such as non-compete obligations for the seller, restrictions on selling remaining shares, the purchaser's right of first refusal, and information rights.

While the agreement itself is straightforward and not unique to Korea, completing the transfer requires specific procedural steps and corporate documentation. Simply signing the agreement does not complete the process—certain procedural and regulatory steps must follow to effectuate the transfer.

Finalizing a (non-listed) share transfer in Korea involves the following:

1. **Price and Share Agreement**: Agree on the price per share and the number and class of shares to be transferred.

2. **Check Restrictions and Approvals**: Review any restrictions or required approvals, such as board resolutions, investor consents, or permits, and conduct due diligence as needed.

3. **Execute the Share Transfer Agreement**: Draft and sign the agreement to formalize the terms.

4. **Wire Payment**: Transfer the purchase price to the seller's designated account.

5. **Update the Shareholder Registry**: Ensure the shareholder registry reflects the new ownership and notify relevant parties as required.

6. **Handle Tax Filings and Payments**: The seller is responsible for paying the securities transaction tax and transfer income tax, along with filing the appropriate documentation.

Unless additional complexities such as external investors or license transfers arise, the process is generally straightforward. Compliance with these procedural steps ensures the share transfer is legally valid and enforceable under Korean law.

4. SHARE SUBSCRIPTION AGREEMENT / SHAREHOLDERS' AGREEMENT / INVESTMENT AGREEMENT

A **share subscription agreement** differs from a share transfer agreement in that it involves the issuance of new shares, injecting fresh capital into the company. In contrast, share transfer agreements involve the exchange of existing shares between shareholders without adding new capital. The core elements of a share subscription agreement include the number and types of shares to be issued (e.g., common or preferred) and the subscription price. These commercial terms are complemented by provisions on representations and warranties, conditions precedent, and payment terms at closing.

In early-stage investment rounds, shareholder rights such as the right of first refusal (ROFR), tag-along rights, information rights, and consent rights are often incorporated into the share subscription agreement itself. These agreements, frequently referred to as i**nvestment agreements**, serve to safeguard investors' interests. For companies with multiple rounds of investors, a separate **shareholders' agreement** may be employed to organize and document rights across all shareholders.

A useful resource for navigating these agreements is the investment agreement template provided by the Korea Venture Capital Association (KVCA), which functions similarly to the NVCA templates widely used in the U.S. While KVCA templates are typically more concise than their U.S. counterparts, they serve as an excellent starting point for drafting and negotiating share subscription agreements.

While the concepts in these agreements mirror those found in U.S. templates, the distinction lies in the procedural steps and corporate documentation needed to complete a share subscription. Once there is a general alignment on the price and number of shares to be issued, the process includes the following steps:

1. Obtain Consent from Existing Shareholders: Ensure compliance with any preemptive rights or required approvals.

2. Execute the Share Subscription Agreement: Formalize the terms through mutual agreement.

3. Pass Required Resolutions: Convene a board or shareholders' meeting to approve the issuance of new shares.

4. Make Announcements and Notifications: Fulfill statutory requirements for announcements, individual notifications.

5. Allocate Shares and Finalize the Subscription: Assign the shares to the subscribing investors.

6. Deposit Investment Funds: Ensure the subscription funds are deposited in the company's designated account.

7. Update the Corporate Registry: Reflect the paid-in capital increase in the corporate registry.

A judicial scrivener often assists with steps 3 to 5, preparing the required resolutions and filing the updated corporate registry. Once the process is complete, the investor is provided with the updated corporate registry, shareholder registry, and a certificate of non-issuance of share certificates. These documents confirm the completion of the subscription and the allocation of shares.

5. LICENSING AGREEMENT

Licensing agreements, which grant rights to intellectual property (IP) in exchange for royalties, are structured similarly to those in other jurisdictions. These agreements focus on defining the IP, specifying the scope of the license, outlining royalty arrangements, and addressing sub-licensing rights. While the general framework is familiar, nuances in local resources and procedures shape the way these agreements are managed and enforced.

Clearly defining the licensed IP is critical. Whether the license is exclusive or non-exclusive, and the specific field of use or geographical territory it covers, must be stated explicitly. Ambiguities in scope can lead to disputes, making detailed drafting essential. Equally important is the royalty structure, which should clarify whether payments are fixed, based on sales, or a combination of both. For agreements involving sales-based royalties, incorporating mechanisms such as audit rights ensures transparency and fairness between the licensor and licensee. Sub-licensing is another vital consideration. Whether the licensee is permitted to grant sub-licenses must be explicitly addressed, as this can significantly impact the licensor's control over their intellectual property.

For practitioners drafting or reviewing these agreements, several resources are particularly helpful. The Korea Intellectual Property Rights Information Service (KIPRIS) offers a robust tool for searching registered IP rights, including patents, trademarks, and designs. This platform is invaluable for verifying ownership or assessing potential conflicts during the preparation of licensing contracts. Additionally, the Ministry of Culture, Sports, and Tourism provides standardized licensing templates, which are available on their website (www.mcst.go.kr). These templates streamline the drafting process and ensure compliance with local regulations, making them an excellent starting point for legal professionals.

In disputes arising from licensing agreements, mediation by the Korea Copyright Commission (KCC) offers a practical alternative to litigation. Established under the Copyright Act, the KCC facilitates a unique mediation process designed to resolve copyright disputes efficiently and cost-effectively. Including a mediation clause referencing the KCC in licensing agreements is common practice, reflecting its reputation as a reliable and expedient forum for resolving IP-related conflicts. Beyond dispute resolution, the KCC plays a broader role in supporting copyright registration, policy development, and research, contributing to the country's intellectual property ecosystem.

6. DATA PROCESS AGREEMENT

Data Processing Agreements (DPAs) in Korea share common elements with those in other jurisdictions, typically covering the definition and scope of data, purpose of data processing, security measures, compensation, and regulations for data management and cross-border transfers.

What distinguishes Korean DPAs are the specific terms based on local regulations, particularly the Personal Information Protection Act (PIPA, 개인정보보호법) and its enforcement decrees. Compliance with PIPA and related guidelines is mandatory. The Personal Information Protection Commission (PIPC, 개인정보보호위원회), operating under the Prime Minister's office, serves as the primary authority overseeing personal information protection. It develops privacy policies, enforces compliance, and mediates disputes through the Personal Information Dispute Mediation Committee (개인정보분쟁조정위원회). This committee, composed of experts in law, IT, and consumer protection, offers an efficient mechanism for resolving privacy-related conflicts. If both parties accept the committee's proposed resolution, it becomes legally binding, providing an alternative to lengthy litigation.

For legal professionals, the PIPC's website (www.pipc.go.kr) offers practical resources, including standard templates and compliance guides. These tools help ensure adherence to privacy regulations and offer best practices for managing data processors, conducting training, and implementing robust data protection measures.

> 본 표준 개인정보처리위탁 계약서는 「개인정보 보호법」 제26조제1항에 따라 위탁 계약에 있어 개인정보 처리에 관하여 문서로 정하여야 하는 최소한의 사항을 표준적으로 제시한 것으로서, 위탁계약이나 위탁업무의 내용 등에 따라 세부적인 내용은 달라질 수 있습니다.
>
> 개인정보처리업무를 위탁하거나 위탁업무에 개인정보 처리가 포함된 경우에는 본 표준 개인정보처리위탁 계약서의 내용을 위탁계약서에 첨부하거나 반영하여 사용하실 수 있습니다.

<u>표준 개인정보처리위탁 계약서(안)</u>

OOO(이하 "위탁자"이라 한다)과 △△△(이하 "수탁자"이라 한다)는 "위탁자"의 개인정보 처리업무를 "수탁자"에게 위탁함에 있어 다음과 같은 내용으로 본 업무위탁계약을 체결한다.

(Source: Cover of the DPA template offered by the PIPC)

7. REAL ESTATE CONTRACTS

Real estate transactions, whether buying, selling, or leasing, are typically conducted using standardized templates provided by the Korea Association of Realtors. Realtors handle the entire process—from property inspections to closing—without requiring escrow agents, or other service providers commonly seen in other jurisdictions. For residential properties, a three-page checklist called the *Confirmation and Explanation of Real Estate Details* (중개대상물 확인설명서), prepared by the realtor, serves in place of formal inspection reports. Escrow accounts are rarely used. The essential documents for closing generally consist of a one-page transfer agreement, the three-page inspection checklist, and a power of attorney (POA) from the seller for the title transfer. Realtor fees are capped at 0.7% of the transaction value but are often negotiated to 0.5%, with each party paying their own agent's fee.

부 동 산 매 매 계 약 서

매도인과 매수인 쌍방은 아래 표시 부동산에 관하여 다음 계약 내용과 같이 매매계약을 체결한다.

1. 부동산의 표시

소 재 지						
토 지	지 목		대지권		면 적	㎡
건 물	구조·용도		면 적			㎡

2. 계약내용

제 1 조 (목적) 위 부동산의 매매에 대하여 매도인과 매수인은 합의에 의하여 매매대금을 아래와 같이 지불하기로 한다.

매매대금	금 원정(₩)		
계 약 금	금 원정은 계약시에 지불하고 영수함. 영수자(인)		
융 자 금	금 원정(은행)을 승계키로 한다.	**임대보증금**	총 원정을 승계키로 한다.
중 도 금	금 원정은 년 월 일에 지불하며		
	금 원정은 년 월 일에 지불한다.		
잔 금	금 원정은 년 월 일에 지불한다.		

제 2 조 (소유권 이전 등) 매도인은 매매대금의 잔금 수령과 동시에 매수인에게 소유권이전등기에 필요한 모든 서류를 교부하고 등기절차에 협력하며, 위 부동산의 인도일은 ____년____월____일로 한다.

제 3 조 (제한물권 등의 소멸) 매도인은 위의 부동산에 설정된 저당권, 지상권, 임차권 등 소유권의 행사를 제한하는 사유가 있거나, 조세공과 기타 부담금의 미납금 등이 있을 때에는 잔금 수수일까지 그 권리의 하자 및 부담 등을 제거하여 완전한 소유권을 매수인에게 이전한다. 다만, 승계하기로 합의하는 권리 및 금액은 그러하지 아니하다.

제 4 조 (지방세 등) 위 부동산에 관하여 발생한 수익의 귀속과 제세공과금 등의 부담은 위 부동산의 인도일을 기준으로 하되, 지방세의 납부의무 및 납부책임은 지방세법의 규정에 의한다.

제 5 조 (계약의 해제) 매수인이 매도인에게 중도금(중도금이 없을때에는 잔금)을 지불하기 전까지 매도인은 계약금의 배액을 상환하고, 매수인은 계약금을 포기하고 본 계약을 해제할 수 있다.

제 6 조 (채무불이행과 손해배상) 매도자 또는 매수자가 본 계약상의 내용에 대하여 불이행이 있을 경우 그 상대방은 불이행한자에 대하여 서면으로 최고하고 계약을 해제할 수 있다. 그리고 계약당사자는 계약해제에 따른 손해배상을 각각 상대방에게 청구할 수 있다.

제 7 조 (중개수수료) 부동산중개업자는 매도인 또는 매수인의 본 계약 불이행에 대하여 책임을 지지 않는다. 또한, 중개수수료는 본 계약체결과 동시에 계약 당사자 쌍방이 각각 지불하며, 중개업자의 고의나 과실없이 본 계약이 무효·취소 또는 해약되어도 중개수수료는 지급한다. 공동 중개인 경우에 매도인과 매수인은 자신이 중개 의뢰한 중개업자에게 각각 중개수수료를 지급한다.(중개수수료는 거래가액의 ____%로 한다.)

제 8 조 (중개대상물확인·설명서 교부등)중개업자는 중개대상물 확인·설명서를 작성하고 업무보증관계증서(공제증서등) 사본을 첨부하여 ____년 월 일 거래당사자 쌍방에게 교부한다.

특약사항 --

(Source: Cover of the DPA template offered by the PIPC)

A critical aspect of any real estate transaction is verifying the real estate registry (부동산 등기부), which functions much like a birth certificate for the property, detailing its official title and ownership. Realtors are responsible for reviewing this document before closing, but it is also accessible online at www.iros.go.kr for direct verification.

Jeonse (전세) system stands out as a unique rental structure. Under *Jeonse*, tenants deposit a large sum—often close to the property's value—in exchange for living in the property rent-free for a fixed term. At the end of the term, the deposit is returned in full. While this system effectively operates as a private loan to the owner, it carries risks, especially if the owner becomes insolvent. Therefore, tenants must carefully verify the property's value and any existing mortgages before entering into a *Jeonse* agreement. Another concept in Korean real estate is *Geunjeodang* (근저당), a form of mortgage security. Unlike typical mortgages, *Geunjeodang* secures a debt but remains valid even if the debt amount is reduced to zero during its term. This mechanism ensures continued security for creditors. Standardized templates for both *Jeonse* and *Geunjeodang* agreements simplify the process. Banks usually provide *Geunjeodang* contracts, while realtors handle *Jeonse* contracts, streamlining compliance with industry practices.

8. STANDARDIZED CONTRACTS AND OTHERS

For contracts such as standardized terms and conditions (약관), subcontract agreements (하도급계약), franchise agreements (가맹계약), distribution agreements (유통계약), and agency agreements (대리점계약), the Korea Fair Trade Commission (KFTC) provides best practice templates accessible on its website. These templates, tailored to various industries, are designed to mitigate risks and protect parties with less bargaining power by ensuring compliance with competition laws. The KFTC even offers specific templates for niche areas, such as the *Standard Terms for Golf Course Use,* which outline conditions like reservation deposit limits (up to 10% of the total fee), refund terms, and prohibitions on gambling during play.

골프장이용 표준약관

공정거래위원회
표준약관 제10033호
(2022. 12. 9. 개정)

제1조(목적) 이 약관은 골프장사업자(이하 "사업자"라 한다)와 골프장의 시설물을 이용하려는 모든 내장객(이하 "이용자"라 한다)간의 골프장 시설물 이용 및 이에 따르는 책임에 관한 사항을 규정함을 목적으로 한다.

(Source: Cover of the Standardized Terms for Golf Course Use offered by the KFTC)

The purpose of these templates is to promote fairness and safeguard vulnerable parties in contractual relationships. For example, the *Standard Subcontract Agreement* aligns with the Subcontracting Act to address industry-specific needs and reduce legal risks, while the *Standard Franchise Agreement* reflects the Franchise Business Act, ensuring balanced practices in franchising. Similarly, the *Standard Distribution Agreement* is guided by the Large-Scale Retail Business Act to prevent disputes and maintain compliance.

For legal counsels, these templates provide a practical foundation for drafting contracts and can be used as leverage during negotiations to advocate for fairer terms. By referencing these established standards, counsels can promote transparency, fairness, and legal compliance while simplifying the contract process. These resources ultimately support the creation of balanced agreements that protect less powerful parties and foster sound trading practices.

LIST OF USEFUL RESOURCES

1. **Standard Employment Contract Templates:**
   Provided by the Ministry of Employment and Labor (MOEL)
   https://www.moel.go.kr/mainpop2.do
2. **Standard Non-Disclosure Agreement(NDA) Templates and Guidance:**
   Provided by the Trade Secret Protection Center, Korean Intellectual Property Office (KIPO).
   https://www.tradesecret.or.kr/bbs/standard.do?gb=241
3. **Investment Agreement Templates:**
   Provided by the Korea Venture Capital Association (KVCA).
   https://www.kvca.or.kr/Program/board/list.html?a_gb=board&a_cd=12&a_item=0&sm=4_3
4. **Copyright Licensing Templates:**
   Provided by the Ministry of Culture, Sports, and Tourism

(MCST).
https://www.mcst.go.kr/kor/s_data/generalData/dataView.jsp?pSeq=41&pMenuCD=0405050000&pCurrentPage=1&pType=&pSearchType=01&pSearchWord=

5. **Standard Data Processing Agreement (DPA) Templates and Guidance:**
   Provided by the Personal Information Protection Commission (PIPC).
   https://www.privacy.go.kr/front/bbs/bbsView.do?bbsNo=BBSMSTR_000000000048&bbscttNo=11932
6. **Real Estate Registry Access:** https://www.iros.go.kr/index.jsp
7. **Best Practice Templates for Standardized Terms and Conditions, Subcontract, Franchise, Distribution, and Agency Agreements**:
   Provided by the Korea Fair Trade Commission (KFTC).
   https://www.ftc.go.kr/www/cop/bbs/selectBoardList.do?key=201&bbsId=BBSMSTR_000000002320&bbsTyCode=BBST01

CLOSING

This book was written as a field manual to make Korean law more accessible and practical for foreign legal professionals. It provides a broad overview of the legal landscape along with focused guidance on key areas such as statutes, procedures, corporate governance, and contracts.

As my career has shown, legal practice is not just about knowing laws—it's about understanding the context in which they operate and working with the people who rely on them. In some ways, lawyers are like the modern-day sorcerers Yuval Harari describes, crafting and sustaining the shared beliefs that underpin concepts like corporations, contracts, and legal systems. Korean law, like any other, is built on these shared understandings. By familiarizing yourself with its terms and processes, you can connect global legal principles to the specifics of this jurisdiction.

This book is a starting point. It is designed to help you approach Korean law with clarity and purpose, bridging gaps and fostering collaboration with Korean lawyers and business stakeholders. Thank you for including this resource in your professional journey. I hope it serves you well as you deepen your understanding of Korean legal practice.

ABOUT THE AUTHOR

Jinny Suh (Korean name: 서여진) is a dual-licensed attorney in Korea and New York with over 18 years of experience spanning private practice, entrepreneurship, and in-house counsel roles at a global consulting firm. She holds law degrees from UCLA and Seoul National University and has built her career advising clients at Kim & Chang, running her own legal practice, and guiding legal strategies within multinational corporations. As a generalist in an increasingly specialized legal environment, Jinny connects the dots across diverse legal domains, offering both a broad understanding of Korea's legal framework and actionable tools for foreign professionals. (Linkedin: https://www.linkedin.com/in/jinnysuh00/)

Made in the USA
Columbia, SC
07 June 2025